Hillsdale Community Church

In this book are some large words which should not be used with young children. Story number 35 should not be used. In each story, it is always best to tell it to the children rather than to read it directly from the book. This book can serve as a guide for the teacher to use her own way of telling the story and making it simple enough for the children to understand the meaning without using misunderstood theological terms.

Hillsdale Community Church
United Church of Christ
6948 SW Capitol Hwy.
Portland, OR 97219

THE LIVING STORY OF Jesus

MATTHEW • MARK • LUKE • JOHN

Regal Books, G/L Publications
Glendale, California, U.S.A.

Co-published by

Tyndale House, Publishers
Wheaton, Illinois, U.S.A.

Before the story begins
1 In the beginning
2 Surprised in the sanctuary
3 A secret message
4 Arrival of the messenger
5 Best news ever
6 Expectations rewarded
7 Visit of the star-watchers
8 Escape
9 Frantic searchers
10 Man with a mission
11 Voice from heaven
12 Put to the test
13 Greater than this
14 Best for the last
15 Coins, cattle and confusion
16 A night visitor
17 A thirsty woman
18 A determined father
19 A furious crowd
20 Deserted boats and nets
21 Much in demand
22 The sick and the sinful
23 Poolside miracle
24 Miracle seekers
25 The inner circle
26 Ways of happiness and love
27 Ways for worriers
28 Ways of prayer
29 Amazing faith
30 Big question

© Copyright 1967
by Gospel Light Publications

Library of Congress
Catalog Card
No.: 67-30247

Printed in U.S.A.

31	Much forgiven, much loved	62	Marketplace, or temple?
32	Listen! Hear!	63	Unanswered question
33	From panic to peace	64	Trick questions
34	Desperate	65	As lightning flashes
35	Birthday party murder	66	Signals
36	More than enough	67	Blood money
37	Rescue at dawn	68	Supper for thirteen men
38	People, people, people!	69	A night to remember
39	Extraordinary picnic	70	Final instructions
40	The touch that heals	71	Heavenly plans
41	Sworn to secrecy	72	Time running out
42	Time for teaching and taxes	73	Agony in a garden
43	Seventy times seven	74	Arrested and deserted
44	Many opinions	75	Guilty!
45	Seeing is believing	76	Sound of the rooster
46	All for his own	77	Field of blood
47	Which neighbors?	78	Nothing more to say
48	Upset over details	79	Exchanged for a murderer
49	Proof enough	80	Place of the skull
50	Found!	81	Between two robbers
51	More than enough proof	82	Darkness, death and destruction
52	Death plot	83	Spices and tender hands
53	Only one	84	Broken seal
54	To boasters	85	First to know
55	Entrance requirements	86	Great discovery
56	Beginning the dreadful journey	87	Plans for a reunion
57	Change of heart	88	Unforgettable journey
58	Faith enough	89	Without a doubt
59	Wanted!	90	Breakfast on the beach
60	Dinner party at Bethany	91	Plans revealed
61	All according to plan	92	The reason why

BEFORE THE STORY BEGINS

In this book you can read the story of Jesus, from the time He came to earth until He returned to His Father in heaven.

What Jesus did and said was written by four men who knew Him well. Today we refer to them as the four Gospel writers—Matthew, Mark, Luke and John. To read the complete story of Jesus' life here on earth we must read what each of the four men wrote. For instance, not all of these men wrote about the same events. Matthew and Luke are the only writers to tell us of Jesus' birth. No one but John tells about Jesus raising Lazarus from the dead, and about Jesus' breakfast beside the lake with His disciples after He arose from the dead. Matthew, Mark and Luke are the three who wrote about the last Passover supper Jesus had with His disciples in the upper room. But all four wrote of Jesus' crucifixion, His death and His resurrection.

If Jesus were here to talk with us now, He would speak in the language we use. So in this book we are telling the wonderful story of Jesus in today's language. And we are using the words of *Living Gospels*, a modern-language paraphrase written and published by Kenneth N. Taylor (Tyndale House, 1966).

We have made a few changes from the words of *Living Gospels*. In the portions from the Gospel of John that tell of the death and resurrection of Christ we have changed the pronouns "I" or "me" to "he" or "him" for sake of clarity. In other places we have added phrases to show the passage of time, change of location or the person speaking. To make the passing of time clear we have included some dates—the year, the month, the day, and even the hour. While these dates are not absolute, they are believed by biblical scholars* to be quite probable.

The idea of making one continuous story of the four Gospels is not new. The first man to try this was Tatian. He completed his story about 120 years after Jesus' resurrection and return to heaven. Tatian's story was known as the *Diatessaron*, which was read again and again for several hundred years in the churches of Syria.

Today you will enjoy reading from this book the events of Jesus' life on earth. And as you read, remember that this book tells the amazing story of Jesus—"So that you will believe that He is the Messiah, the Son of God, and that believing in Him you will have life." (John 20:31)

THE EDITORS

* As published in the *Holy Bible, the Berkeley Version* (Zondervan Publishing House, © 1946. Used by permission).

Before anything else existed, there was Christ with God. He has always been alive and is Himself God. He created everything there is—nothing exists that He didn't make. Eternal life is in Him, and this life gives light to all mankind. His life is the light that shines through the darkness—and the darkness can never extinguish it.

Several people have already written accounts of Christ's life on earth, and have used as their source material the reports circulating among us from the early disciples and other eyewitnesses. However, it occurred to me that it would be well to recheck all these accounts from first to last, and after thorough investigation, to pass this summary on to you so that you may be reassured of the truth of all you were taught.

From Luke 1:1-4; John 1:1-5

1
IN THE BEGINNING

2
SURPRISED IN THE SANCTUARY
About 6 B.C.

In the book written by the prophet Isaiah, God announced that He would send His Son to earth, and that a special messenger would come first to prepare the world for His arrival. "This messenger will live out in the barren wilderness," Isaiah said, "and will proclaim that everyone must straighten out his life to be ready for the Lord's arrival."

This messenger was John the Baptist.

My story of this messenger begins with a Jewish priest, Zacharias, who lived when Herod was king of Judea. Zacharias was a member of the Abijah division of the Temple service corps. His wife Elizabeth was also a member of the priest tribe of the Jews, being a descendant of Aaron. Zacharias and Elizabeth were godly folk, careful to obey all of God's laws—in spirit as well as in letter. But they had no children, for Elizabeth was barren; and now they were very old.

One day as Zacharias was going about his work in the Temple—for his division was on duty that week—the honor fell to him by lot to enter the inner sanctuary and burn incense before the Lord. Meanwhile, a great crowd stood outside in the Temple court, praying as they always did during that part of the service when the incense was being burned. Zacharias was in the sanctuary when suddenly an angel appeared, standing to the right of the altar of incense! Zacharias was startled and terrified.

But the angel said, "Don't be afraid, Zacharias! For I have come to tell you that God has heard your prayer, and your wife, Elizabeth, will bear you a son! And you are to name him John! You will both have great joy and gladness at his birth, and many will rejoice with you. For he will be one of the Lord's great men. He must never touch wine or strong drink—and he will be filled with the Holy Spirit, even from before his birth! And he will persuade many a Jew to turn to the Lord his God. He will be a man of rugged spirit and power, like Elijah, the prophet of old; and he will precede the coming of the Messiah, preparing the people for His arrival. He will teach them to love the Lord, just as their ancestors did, and to live as godly men."

Zacharias said to the angel, "But how can I be sure of this? For I am an old man now, and my wife is also well along in years."

Then the angel said, "I am Gabriel! I stand in the very presence of God. It was He who sent me to bring you this good news! And now because you haven't believed me, you are to be stricken silent, unable to speak until the child is born. For my words will certainly come true at the proper time!"

Meanwhile, the crowds outside were waiting for Zacharias to come out, and wondered why he was taking so long. When he finally appeared, he couldn't speak to them; and they realized from his gestures that he must have seen a vision in the Temple. He then fulfilled the remaining days of his Temple duties and returned home.

Soon afterwards Elizabeth his wife became pregnant, and went into seclusion for five months. "How kind the Lord is," she exclaimed, "to take away my disgrace of having no children!"

From Mark 1:2-4; Luke 1:5-25

3
A SECRET MESSAGE
About March, 5 B.C.

The following month God sent the angel Gabriel to Nazareth, a village in Galilee, to a virgin named Mary, engaged to be married to a man named Joseph, a descendant of King David. Gabriel appeared to her and said, "Congratulations, favored lady! The Lord is with you!" Confused and disturbed, she tried to think what he could mean.

"Don't be frightened, Mary," the angel said, "for God has decided to wonderfully bless you! Very soon now, you will become pregnant and have a baby boy, and you are to name Him 'Jesus.' He shall be very great and shall be called the Son of God. And the Lord God shall give Him the throne of His ancestor David. And He shall reign over Israel forever; His Kingdom shall never end!"

Mary asked the angel, "But how can I have a baby? I am a virgin."

The angel replied, "The Holy Spirit shall come upon you, and the power of God shall overshadow you; so the baby born to you will be utterly holy—the Son of God. Furthermore, six months ago your cousin Elizabeth—'the barren one,' they called her—became pregnant in her old age! For every promise from God shall surely come true."

Mary said, "I am the Lord's servant, and I am willing to do whatever He says. May everything come true as you have told me." And then the angel disappeared.

A few days later Mary hurried to the highlands of Judea to the town where Zacharias lived, to visit Elizabeth. At the sound of Mary's greeting, Elizabeth's child leaped within her and she was filled with the Holy Spirit!

She gave a glad cry and exclaimed to Mary, "You are favored by God above all other women, and your child is

destined for God's mightiest praise. What an honor this is, that the mother of my Lord should visit me! When you came in and greeted me, the instant I heard your voice, my baby moved in me for joy! You believed that God would do what He said; that is why He has given you this wonderful blessing."

Mary responded, "Oh, how I praise the Lord! How I rejoice in God my Savior! For He took notice of His lowly servant girl, and now generation after generation forever shall call me blest of God! For He, the mighty Holy One, has done great things to me. His mercy goes on from generation to generation to all who reverence Him. How powerful is His mighty arm! How He scatters the proud and haughty ones! He has torn princes from their thrones and exalted the lowly. He has satisfied the hungry hearts and sent the rich away with empty hands. And how He has helped His servant Israel! He has not forgotten His promise to be merciful. For He promised our fathers—Abraham and his children—to be merciful to them forever."

Mary stayed with Elizabeth about three months and then went back to her own home.

From Luke 1:26-56

4
ARRIVAL OF THE MESSENGER
About June, 5 B.C.

By now Elizabeth's waiting was over, for the time had come for the baby to be born—and it was a boy! The word spread quickly to her neighbors and relatives of how kind the Lord had been to her, and everyone rejoiced.

When the baby was eight days old, all the relatives and friends came for the circumcision ceremony. They all assumed the baby's name would be Zacharias, after his father. But Elizabeth said, "No! He must be named John!"

"What?" they exclaimed. "There is no one in all your family by that name!"

So they asked the baby's father, talking to him by gestures. He motioned for a piece of paper and to everyone's surprise wrote, "His name is John!" Instantly Zacharias could speak again, and he began praising God!

Wonder fell upon the whole neighborhood, and the news of what had happened spread through the Judean hills. And everyone who heard about it thought long thoughts and asked, "I wonder what this child will turn out to be? The hand of the Lord is surely upon him in some special way."

Then his father Zacharias was filled with the Holy Spirit and gave this prophecy:

"And you, my little son, shall be called the prophet of the glorious God, for you will prepare the way for the Messiah. You will tell His people how to find salvation by forgiveness of their sins. All this will be because the mercy of our God is very tender, and heaven's dawn is about to break upon us, to give light to those who sit in darkness and death's shadow, and to guide us to the path of peace."

The little boy greatly loved God. When he grew up, he lived out in the lonely wilderness until he began his public ministry to Israel.

From Luke 1:57-67, 76-80

5
BEST NEWS EVER
About December, 5 B.C.

About that time Caesar Augustus, the Roman Emperor, decreed that a census should be taken throughout the empire. This census was taken when Quirinius was governor of Syria. Everyone was required to return to his ancestral home for the registration. And because Joseph was a member of the royal line, he had to go to Bethlehem in Judea, King David's ancient home—journeying there from the Galilean city of Nazareth. He took with him Mary, who was obviously pregnant by that time.

And while they were there, the time came for her baby to be born; and she gave birth to her first child, a son. She wrapped Him in a blanket and laid Him in a manger, because there was no room for them in the village inn.

That night some shepherds were in the fields outside the village, guarding their flocks of sheep. Suddenly an angel appeared among them, and the landscape shone bright with the glory of the Lord. They were badly frightened, but the angel reassured them. "Don't be afraid!" he said. "I bring you the most joyful news ever announced, and it is for everyone! The Savior—yes, the Messiah, the Lord—has been born tonight in Bethlehem! How will you recognize Him? You will find a baby wrapped in a blanket, lying in a manger!"

Suddenly, the angel was joined by a vast host of others—the armies of heaven—praising God: "Glory to God in the highest heaven," they sang, "and peace on earth for all those pleasing Him."

When this great army of angels had returned to heaven, the shepherds said to each other, "Come on! Let's go to Bethlehem! Let's see this wonderful thing that has happened, which the Lord has told us about." They ran to the village and found their way to Mary and Joseph. And there was the Baby, lying in the manger!

The shepherds told everyone what had happened and what the angel had said to them about this child. Everyone who heard the shepherds' story expressed aston-

ishment, but Mary quietly treasured all these things in her heart and often thought about them. Then the shepherds went back to their fields and flocks again, praising God for the visit of the angels and because they had seen the child, just as the angel had told them they would.

Eight days later at the baby's circumcision ceremony, He was named Jesus, the name given Him by the angel before He was even conceived.

From Luke 2:1-21

6
EXPECTATIONS REWARDED
January - February, 4 B.C.

When the time came for Mary's purification offering at the Temple (as required by the laws of Moses after the birth of a child) Jesus' parents took Him to Jerusalem to present Him to the Lord. At that time Jesus' parents also offered their sacrifice for purification. ("Either a pair of turtledoves or two young pigeons" was the legal requirement.)

That day a man named Simeon, who lived in Jerusalem, was in the Temple. He was a good man, very devout, filled with the Holy Spirit and constantly expecting the Messiah to come soon. For the Holy Spirit had revealed to him that he would not die until he had seen Him—God's anointed King. The Holy Spirit had impelled him to go to the Temple that day; and so, when Mary and Joseph arrived to present the baby Jesus to the Lord in obedience to the law, Simeon was there and took Him in his arms, praising God.

"Lord," he said, "now I can die content! For I have seen Him as You promised me I would! I have seen the Savior You have given to the world! He is the Light that will shine upon the nations, and He will be the glory of Your people Israel!"

Joseph and Mary just stood there, marveling at what was being said about Jesus. Simeon blessed them but then said to Mary, His mother, "A sword shall pierce your soul, for this child shall be rejected by many in Israel, and this to their undoing. But He will be the greatest joy of many others. And the deepest thoughts of many hearts shall be revealed."

Anna, a prophetess, was also there in the Temple that day. She was the daughter of Phanuel, of the Jewish tribe of Asher, and was very old, for she had been a widow for 84 years following seven years of marriage. She never left the Temple but stayed there night and day, worshiping God by praying, and often going without food. She came along just as Simeon was talking with Mary and Joseph, and she also began thanking God and publicly proclaiming the Messiah's arrival to everyone in Jerusalem who had been awaiting the coming of the Savior.

From Luke 2:22, 24-38

7
VISIT OF THE STAR-WATCHERS
About 2 B.C.

During the reign of King Herod, some astrologers from eastern lands arrived in Jerusalem, asking, "Where is the newborn King of the Jews? for we have seen His star in far-off eastern lands, and have come to worship Him."

King Herod was deeply disturbed by their question, and all Jerusalem was filled with rumors. He called a meeting of all the Jewish religious leaders. "Did the prophets tell us where the Messiah would be born?" he asked.

"Yes, in Bethlehem," they said, "for this is what the prophet Micah wrote: 'O little town of Bethlehem, you are not just an unimportant Judean village, for a Governor shall rise from you to rule My people Israel.'"

Then Herod sent a secret message to the astrologers, asking them to come see him; and he found out from them the exact time of the star's first appearance. "Go to Bethlehem," he told them, "and search for the child. And when you find Him, come back and tell me, so that I can worship Him too!" The astrologers listened and then left. And look! The star appeared again, standing over Bethlehem. Their joy knew no bounds! Entering the house where the baby and Mary His mother were, they fell to the floor before Him, worshiping. Then they opened their presents and gave Him gold, frankincense and myrrh.

And when they returned to their own land, they didn't go through Jerusalem to report to Herod, for God had warned them in a dream to go home another way.

From Matthew 2:1-12

After the wise men were gone, Joseph dreamed an angel of the Lord appeared to him. "Get up and flee to Egypt with the Baby and His mother," the angel said, "and stay there until I tell you to return, for King Herod is going to try to kill the child." That same night Joseph left for Egypt with Mary and the Baby and stayed there until King Herod's death. This fulfilled the prophet's prediction, "I have called My Son from Egypt."

Herod was furious when he realized that the astrologers had deceived him. Sending soldiers to Bethlehem, he ordered them to kill every baby boy two years old and under, both in the town and on the nearby farms, for the astrologers had told him the star first appeared to them two years before.

This brutal action of Herod's fulfilled the prophecy of Jeremiah, "Screams of anguish come from Ramah, weeping unrestrained; Rachel weeping for her children, uncomforted—for they are dead."

When Herod died, an angel of the Lord appeared in a dream to Joseph in Egypt, and told him, "Arise and take the Baby and His mother back to Israel, for those who sought to kill the Child are dead."

So he returned immediately to Israel with Jesus and His mother. But on the way he was frightened to learn that the new king was Herod's son, Archelaus. Then, in another dream, he was warned not to go to Jerusalem, so they went to Galilee instead and lived in Nazareth. This fulfilled the prediction of the prophets concerning the Messiah, "He shall be called a Nazarene."

From Matthew 2:13-23

8
ESCAPE

9
FRANTIC SEARCHERS
April, A.D. 8 or 9

In the city of Nazareth the child Jesus became a strong, robust lad, and was known for wisdom beyond His years; and God poured out His blessings on Him.

When Jesus was 12 years old, He accompanied His parents to Jerusalem for the annual Passover Festival, which they attended each year.

After the celebration was over, they started home to Nazareth, but Jesus stayed behind in Jerusalem. They didn't miss Him the first day, for they assumed He was with friends among the other travelers. But when He didn't show up that evening, they started to look for Him among their relatives and friends. When they couldn't find Him, they went back to Jerusalem to search for Him.

Three days later they finally discovered Him in the Temple, sitting among the teachers of Law, discussing deep questions with them and amazing everyone with His understanding and answers. His parents didn't know what to think when they saw Him sitting there with those great men. "Son!" His mother said to Him, "Why have You done this to us? Your father and I have been frantic, searching for You everywhere."

"But why did you need to search?" He asked. "Didn't you realize that I would be here in My Father's House?" But they didn't understand what He meant.

Then He returned to Nazareth with them and was obedient to them; and His mother stored away all these things in her heart. So Jesus grew both tall and wise, and was loved by God and man.

From Luke 2:40-52

10
MAN WITH A MISSION

While Jesus and His family were still living in Nazareth, John the Baptist began preaching out in the Judean wilderness. His clothes were woven from camel's hair and he wore a leather belt; locusts and wild honey were his food.

He went from place to place on both sides of the Jordan River, preaching that people should be baptized to show that they had turned to God and away from their sins in order to be forgiven. And when they confessed their sins, he baptized them in the Jordan River.

Everyone was expecting the Messiah to come soon, and eager to know whether or not John was He. This was the question of the hour, and it was discussed everywhere.

The Jewish leaders sent priests and assistant priests from Jerusalem to ask John whether he claimed to be the Messiah. He denied it flatly. "I am not the Christ," he said.

"Well then, who are you?" they asked. "Are you Elijah?"

"No," he replied.

"Are you the Prophet?"

"No."

"Then who are you? Tell us, so we can give an answer to those who sent us. What do you have to say for yourself?"

He replied, "I am a voice from the barren wilderness, shouting as Isaiah prophesied, 'Get ready for the coming of the Lord!'"

Then those who were sent by the Pharisees asked

him, "If you aren't the Messiah or Elijah or the Prophet, what right do you have to baptize?"

John answered the question by saying, "I baptize only with water; but someone is coming soon who has far higher authority than mine; in fact, I am not worthy of being His slave. He will baptize you ... with the Holy Spirit."

From Matthew 3:1, 6; Mark 1:6; Luke 3:3, 15, 16; John 1:19-25

Soon after, Jesus came from Nazareth in Galilee to be baptized by John in the Jordan. John didn't want to do it. "This isn't proper," he said. "I am the one who needs to be baptized by You."

But Jesus said, "Please do it, for I must do all that is right." So then John baptized Him.

After His baptism, as soon as Jesus came up out of the water, the heavens were opened to Him and He saw the Spirit of God coming down in the form of a dove.

And a voice from heaven said, "This is My beloved Son, and I am very pleased with Him."

From Matthew 3:14-17; Mark 1:9

11
VOICE FROM HEAVEN

About December, A.D. 26 or early part of 27

12 PUT TO THE TEST

Jesus, full of the Holy Spirit, left the Jordan River and was urged by the Spirit out into the barren wastelands of Judea, where Satan tempted Him for 40 days. He ate nothing all that time, and was very hungry.

Satan said, "If you are God's Son, tell this stone to become a loaf of bread."

But Jesus replied, "It is written in the Scriptures, 'Other things in life are more important than bread!'"

Then Satan took Him to a place where he revealed to Jesus all the kingdoms of the world in a moment of time. And the Devil told Him, "I will give You all these splendid kingdoms and their glory—for they are mine to give to anyone I wish—if You will only get down on Your knees before me and worship me."

Jesus replied, "We must worship God, and Him alone. So it is written in the Scriptures."

Then Satan took Him to Jerusalem to a high roof of the Temple and said, "If You are the Son of God, jump off! For the Scriptures say that God will send His angels to guard You and to keep You from crashing to the pavement below!"

Jesus replied, "The Scriptures also say, 'Don't experiment with God's patience!'"

When the Devil had ended all the temptations, he left Jesus for a while and went away.

Jesus was now about 30 years old as He began His public ministry.

From Luke 3:23; 4:1-13

One day as John was standing with two of his disciples, Jesus walked by. John looked at Him intently and then declared, "See! There is the Lamb of God!"

Then two of John's disciples turned and followed Jesus! Jesus looked around and saw them following. "What do you want?" He asked them.

"Sir," they replied, "where do You live?"

"Come and see," He said. So they went with Him to the place where He was staying and were with Him from about four o'clock that afternoon until the evening.

One of these men was Andrew, Simon Peter's brother. (The other man was John, the writer of the Gospel.) Andrew then went to find his brother Peter and told him, "We have found the Messiah!" And he brought him to Jesus.

Jesus looked intently at Peter for a moment and then said, "You are Simon, John's son—but you shall be called Peter, the Rock!"

The next day Jesus decided to go to Galilee. He found Philip and told him, "Come with Me." (Philip was from Bethsaida, Andrew and Peter's home town.)

Then Philip went off to look for Nathanael and told him, "We have found the Messiah!—the very person Moses and the prophets told about! His name is Jesus, the son of Joseph from Nazareth!"

"Nazareth!" exclaimed Nathanael, "Can anything good come from there?"

13

GREATER THAN THIS

"Just come and see for yourself," Philip declared.

As they approached, Jesus said, "Here comes an honest man—a true son of Israel!"

"How do you know what I am like?" Nathanael demanded.

And Jesus replied, "I could see you under that fig tree before Philip found you!"

Nathanael replied, "Sir, You are the Son of God—the King of Israel!"

Jesus asked him, "Do you believe all this just because I told you I had seen you under the fig tree? You will see greater proofs than this!"

From John 1:35-50

14 BEST FOR THE LAST
March, A.D. 27

Two days later Jesus' mother was a guest at a wedding in the village of Cana in Galilee, and Jesus and His disciples were invited too. The wine supply ran out during the festivities, and Jesus' mother came to Him with the problem. Then His mother told the servants, "Do whatever He tells you!"

Six stone waterpots were standing there; they were used for Jewish ceremonial purposes and held perhaps 20 to 30 gallons each. Jesus told the servants to fill them to the brim with water. When this was done He said, "Dip some out and take it to the master of ceremonies."

When the master of ceremonies tasted the water that was now wine, not knowing where it had come from, he called the bridegroom over. "This is wonderful stuff!" he said. "You're different from most hosts! Usually they give out the best wine first; and afterwards when every-

one is full and doesn't care, then they bring out the less expensive brands! But you have kept the best for the last!"

This miracle at Cana in Galilee was Jesus' first demonstration of His heaven-sent power. And His disciples believed that He really was the Messiah.

After the wedding He left for Capernaum for a few days with His mother, brothers, and disciples.

From John 2:1-3, 5-12

15
COINS, CATTLE AND CONFUSION
April or May, A.D. 27

It was time for the Jewish Passover celebration, and Jesus went to Jerusalem. In the Temple area He saw merchants selling cattle, sheep, and doves for sacrifices, and money changers behind their counters. Jesus made a whip from some ropes and chased them all out, and drove out the sheep and oxen, scattered the money changers' coins over the floor and turned over their tables! Then going over to the men selling doves, He told them, "Get these things out of here! Don't turn My Father's House into a market!"

Then His disciples remembered this Old Testament prophecy: "Concern for God's House will be My undoing!"

"What right have You to order them out?" the Jewish leaders demanded. "If You have this authority from God, show us a miracle to prove it."

"All right," Jesus replied, "this is the miracle I will do for you: Destroy this Sanctuary and in three days I will raise it up!"

"What!" they exclaimed. "It took 46 years to build this Temple, and You can do it in three days?"

But by "this Sanctuary," He meant His body. After He came back to life, the disciples remembered His saying this and realized that what He had quoted from the Old Testament really did refer to Him and had come true!

From John 2:13-22

After dark one night a Jewish religious leader named Nicodemus, a member of the sect of the Pharisees, came for an interview with Jesus. "Sir," he said, "we all know that God has sent You to teach us. Your miracles are proof enough of this."

Jesus replied, "With all the earnestness I possess I tell you this: Unless you are born again, you can never get into the Kingdom of God."

"Born again!" exclaimed Nicodemus. "What do You mean? How can an old man go back into his mother's womb and be born again?"

Jesus replied, "What I am telling you so earnestly is

16

A NIGHT VISITOR

this: Unless one is born of water and the Spirit, he cannot enter the Kingdom of God. Men can only reproduce human life, but the Holy Spirit gives you new life from heaven, so don't be surprised at My statement that you must be born again! Just as you can hear the wind but can't tell where it comes from or where it will go next, so it is with the Spirit! We do not know on whom He will next bestow this life from heaven."

"What do You mean?" Nicodemus asked.

Jesus replied, "You, a respected Jewish teacher, and yet you don't understand these things? I am telling you what I know and have seen—and yet you won't believe Me. But if you don't even believe Me when I tell you about such things as these happening here among men, how can you possibly believe if I tell you what is going on in heaven? For only I, the Son of Man, have come to earth and will return to heaven again.

"And as Moses in the wilderness lifted up the image of a bronze serpent on a pole, even so must I be lifted up upon a pole so that anyone who believes in Me will have eternal life. For God loved the world so much that He gave His only Son so that anyone who believes in Him will not perish but have eternal life.

"God did not send His Son into the world to condemn the world, but to save it. There is no eternal doom awaiting those who are trusting Him to save them. But those who don't trust Him have already been tried and condemned for not believing in the only Son of God. Their sentence is based on this fact: that the Light from heaven came into the world, but they loved their former darkness more than the Light, for their deeds were evil. They hated the heavenly Light because they wanted to sin in the darkness. They stayed away from that Light for fear their sins would be exposed and they would be punished. But those doing right come gladly to the Light to let everyone see that they are doing what God wants them to."

From John 3:1-21

Jesus left Judea and returned home to Nazareth in Galilee. On the way He had to go through an area called Samaria.

Around noon, as He approached the village of Sychar, He came to Jacob's Well, located on the parcel of ground Jacob gave to his son Joseph. Jesus was tired from the long walk in the hot sun and sat wearily beside the well. Soon a Samaritan woman came to draw water, and Jesus asked her for a drink. He was alone at the time as His disciples had gone into the village to buy some food. The woman was surprised that a Jew would ask a "despised Samaritan" for anything. Usually Jews didn't even speak to them. The woman remarked about this to Jesus.

A THIRSTY WOMAN

January, A.D. 28

He replied, "If you only knew what a wonderful gift God has for you, and who I am, you would ask Me for some *living* water!"

"But You don't have a rope or a bucket," she said, "and this is a very deep well! From where would you get this living water? And besides, are you greater than our ancestor Jacob? How can you offer better water than this which he himself enjoyed, along with his sons and cattle?"

Jesus replied that people soon became thirsty again after drinking that water. "But the water I give them," He said, "becomes a perpetual spring within them, watering them forever with eternal life."

"Please, Sir," the woman said, "give me some of that water! Then I'll never be thirsty again and won't have to make this long trip out here every day."

"Go and get your husband," Jesus told her.

"But I'm not married," the woman replied.

"All too true!" Jesus said, "for you have had five husbands, and you aren't even married to the man you're living with now! You couldn't have spoken a truer word!"

"Sir," the woman said, "You must be a prophet! But say, tell me, why is it you Jews insist that Jerusalem is the only place of worship, while we Samaritans claim it is here at Mount Gerazim, where our ancestors worshiped?"

Jesus replied, "The time is coming, Ma'am, when we will no longer be concerned about whether to worship the Father here or in Jerusalem! For it's not *where* we worship that counts, but *how* we worship—is our worship spiritual and real? Do we have the Holy Spirit's help? For God is Spirit, and we must have His Spirit's help to worship as we should. The Father wants this kind of worship from us. But you Samaritans know so little about Him, worshiping blindly, while we Jews know all about Him, for salvation comes to the world through the Jews."

The woman said, "Well, at least I know that the Messiah will come—the one they call Christ—and when He does, He will explain everything to us."

Then Jesus told her, "I am the Messiah!"

Just then His disciples arrived. They were surprised to find Him talking to a woman, but none of them asked Him why, or what they had been discussing.

Then the woman left her waterpot beside the well and went back to the village and told everyone, "Come and meet a man who told me everything I ever did! Can this be the Messiah?" So the people came streaming from the village to see Him.

Meanwhile, the disciples were urging Jesus to eat. "No," He said, "I have some food you don't know about!"

"Who brought it to Him?" the disciples asked one another.

Then Jesus explained: "My nourishment comes from doing the will of God who sent Me and finishing His work."

Many from that Samaritan village believed He was the Messiah because of the woman's report, "He told me everything I ever did!" So when they saw Him at the well, they begged Him to stay at their village; and He did for two days.

While He was there teaching them, many others believed. Then they said to the woman, "Now we believe because we have heard Him ourselves, not just because of what you told us. He is indeed the Savior of the world."

From John 4:3-34, 39-42

18
A DETERMINED FATHER
Before April, A.D. 28

At the end of the two days' stay Jesus went on into the province of Galilee. And sure enough, the Galileans welcomed Him with open arms, for they had been in Jerusalem at the Passover celebration and had seen some of His miracles.

As Jesus traveled through Galilee He arrived at the town of Cana, where He had turned the water into wine. While He was there, a government official in the city of Capernaum, whose son was very sick, heard that Jesus had come from Judea and was traveling in Galilee. This man went over to Cana, found Jesus, and begged Him to come to Capernaum with him and heal his son, who was now at death's door.

Jesus asked, "Won't any of you believe in Me unless I do more and more miracles?"

But the official pled with Him, "Sir, please come now before my child dies."

Then Jesus told him, "Go back home. Your son is healed!" The man believed Jesus and started home.

While he was on his way, some of his servants met him with the news that all was well—his son had recovered! He asked them when the lad had begun to feel better, and they replied, "Yesterday afternoon at about one o'clock when his fever was suddenly gone!" Then the father realized it was the same moment that Jesus had told him, "Your son is healed." And the officer and his entire household believed that Jesus was the Messiah.

From John 4:43, 45-53

When He came to the village of Nazareth, His boyhood home, He went, as usual, to the synagogue on Saturday, and stood up to read the Scriptures. The book of Isaiah the prophet was handed to Him, and He opened it to the place where it says: "The Spirit of the Lord is upon Me; He has appointed Me to preach Good News to the poor; He has sent Me to announce that captives shall be released and the blind shall see, that the downtrodden shall be freed from their oppressors, and that God is ready to give blessings to all who come to Him."

Then He closed the book and handed it back to the attendant and sat down, while everyone in the synagogue gazed at Him intently. Then He added, "These Scriptures came true today!"

As He made these remarks, the people in the synagogue were filled with sudden fury; and jumping up, they mobbed Him and took Him to the edge of the hill on which the city was built, to push Him over the cliff. But He walked away through the crowd and left them.

From Luke 4:16-21, 28-30

19
A FURIOUS CROWD

20

DESERTED BOATS AND NETS

One day as He was preaching on the shore of Lake Gennesaret, great crowds pressed in on Him to listen to the Word of God. He noticed two empty boats standing at the water's edge, while the fishermen washed their nets. Stepping into one of the boats, Jesus asked Simon (its owner) to push out a little into the water, so that He could sit in the boat and speak to the crowds from there.

When He had finished speaking, He said to Simon, "Now go out where it is deeper and let down your nets and you will catch a lot of fish!"

"Sir," Simon replied, "we worked hard all last night and didn't catch a thing! But if You say so, we'll try again."

And this time their nets were so full that they began

to tear! A shout for help brought their partners in the other boat, and soon both boats were filled with fish and on the verge of sinking!

When Simon Peter realized what had happened, he fell to his knees before Jesus and said, "Oh, Sir, please leave us, for I'm too much of a sinner for You to be around." For he was awestruck by the size of their catch, as were the others with him.

Jesus called out, "Come along with Me and I will show you how to fish for the souls of men!" Immediately they left their nets and followed Him!

A little farther up the beach He saw two other brothers, James and John, sitting in a boat with their father Zebedee, mending their nets; and He called to them to come too. They stopped their work at once, and left their father, and followed Him.

From Matthew 4:19-22; Luke 5:1-9

21 MUCH IN DEMAND

Not long after this Jesus and His companions arrived at the town of Capernaum and on Saturday morning went into the Jewish place of worship—the synagogue—where He preached. The congregation was surprised at His sermon because He spoke as an authority, and didn't try to prove His points by quoting others—quite unlike what they were used to hearing!

Afterwards, when they left the synagogue, He and His disciples went over to Simon and Andrew's home. When they arrived they found Simon's mother-in-law sick in bed with a high fever, and they told Jesus about her right away. He went to her bedside, and as He took her by the hand and helped her to sit up, the fever suddenly left, and she got up and prepared dinner for them!

As the sun went down that evening, all the villagers who had sick people in their homes, no matter what their diseases were, brought them to Jesus; and the touch of His hands healed everyone!

The next morning He was up long before daybreak and went out alone into the wilderness to pray. Later, Simon and the others went out searching for Him and told Him, "Everyone is asking for You."

But He replied, "We must go on to other towns as well and give them My message, too, for that is why I came." So He traveled throughout the province of Galilee, preaching in the synagogues and releasing many from the power of demons.

The report of His miracles spread far beyond the borders of Galilee, so that sick folk were soon coming to be healed from as far away as Syria. They had every kind of illness and pain, or were possessed by demons, or were insane, or paralyzed—and He healed them all.

Once a leper came and knelt in front of Him and begged to be healed. "If You want to, You can make me well again," he pled.

And Jesus, moved with pity, touched him and said, "I want to! Be healed!" And immediately the leprosy was gone—the man was healed!

Jesus then told him sternly, "Go and be examined immediately by the Jewish priest. Don't stop to speak to anyone along the way. Take along the offering prescribed by Moses for a leper who is healed, so that everyone will have proof that you are well again."

But as the man went on his way he began to shout the good news that he was healed; as a result, such throngs soon surrounded Jesus that He couldn't publicly enter a city anywhere, but had to stay out in the barren wastelands. And people from everywhere came to Him there.

From Matthew 4:24; Mark 1:21, 22, 29-31, 35-45; Luke 4:40

Several days later He returned to Capernaum, and the news of His arrival spread quickly through the city. Soon the house where He was staying was so packed with visitors that there wasn't room for another person, not even outside the door. And He preached the Word to them.

Then—look! Some men came carrying a paralyzed man on a sleeping mat. They tried to push through the crowd to Jesus but couldn't reach Him. So they went up

22
THE SICK AND THE SINFUL

on the roof above Him, took off some tiles and lowered the sick man down into the middle of the crowd, still on his sleeping mat, right in front of Jesus!

Seeing their faith, Jesus said to the man, "My friend, your sins are forgiven!"

"Who does this fellow think He is?" the Pharisees and teachers of the Law exclaimed among themselves. "This is blasphemy! Who but God can forgive sins?"

Jesus knew what they were thinking, and He replied, "Why is it blasphemy? Which is easier for Me to do, to say I have forgiven his sins, or to actually heal him? Now I will prove My authority to forgive sin by demonstrating My power to heal disease." Then He said to the paralyzed man, "Get up, roll up your sleeping mat and go on home!"

And immediately, as everyone watched, the man jumped to his feet, picked up his mat and went home praising God!

Everyone present was gripped with awe and fear. And they praised God, remarking over and over again, "We have seen strange things today."

Later on, as Jesus left the town, He saw a tax collector—with the usual reputation for cheating—sitting at a collection booth. The man's name was Levi (known also as Matthew, one of the four Gospel writers). Jesus said to him, "Come and be one of My disciples!" So Levi left everything, sprang up and went with Him!

Soon Levi held a reception in his home, with Jesus as the guest of honor. Many of Levi's fellow tax collectors and other guests were there. But the Pharisees and teachers of the Law complained bitterly to Jesus' disciples about His eating with such notorious sinners. Jesus answered them, "It is the sick who need a doctor, not those in good health! My purpose is to invite sinners to turn from their sins, not to spend My time with those who think themselves already good enough."

From Mark 2:1, 2; Luke 5:18-32

23
POOLSIDE MIRACLE
April, A.D. 28

Afterwards Jesus returned to Jerusalem for one of the Jewish religious holidays. Inside the city near the Sheep Gate was Bethesda Pool, with five covered platforms or porches surrounding it. Crowds of sick folk—lame, blind, or with paralyzed limbs—lay on the platforms waiting for a certain movement of the water, for an angel of the Lord came from time to time and disturbed the water, and the first person to step down into it afterwards was healed!

One of the men lying there had been sick for 38 years. When Jesus saw him and knew how long he had been ill, He asked him, "Would you like to get well?"

"I can't," the sick man said, "for I have no one to help me into the pool at the movement of the water. While I am trying to get there, someone else always gets in ahead of me."

Jesus told him, "Stand up, roll up your sleeping mat and go on home!" Instantly, the man was healed! He rolled up the mat and began walking!

But it was on the Sabbath when this miracle was done. So the Jewish leaders objected! They said to the man who was cured, "You can't work on the Sabbath! It's illegal to carry that sleeping mat!"

"The man who healed me told me to," was his reply.

"Who said such a thing as that?" they demanded.

The man didn't know, and Jesus had disappeared into the crowd. But afterwards Jesus found him in the Temple and told him, "Now you are well; don't sin as you did before, or something even worse may happen to you."

Then the man went to find the Jewish leaders, and told them it was Jesus who had healed him. So they began harassing Jesus as a Sabbath breaker. But Jesus replied, "My Father constantly does good, and I'm following His example!"

On another Sabbath He was in the synagogue teaching, and a man was present whose right hand was de-

May, A.D. 28

formed. The teachers of the Law and the Pharisees watched closely to see whether He would heal the man that day, since it was the Sabbath! For they were eager to find some charge to bring against Him. How well He knew their thoughts! But He said to the man with the deformed hand, "Come and stand here where everyone can see." So he did.

Then Jesus said to the Pharisees and teachers of the Law, "I have a question for you. Is it right to do good on the Sabbath day, or to do harm? To save life, or to destroy it? If you had just one sheep, and it fell into a well on the Sabbath, would you work to rescue it that day? Of course you would! And how much more valuable is a person than a sheep! Yes, it is right to do good on the Sabbath! For I, the Son of Man, am master even of the Sabbath."

He looked around at them one by one and then said to the man, "Stretch out your arm!" And as he did, his hand became normal, just like the other one! At this, the enemies of Jesus were wild with rage and began to plot His murder.

From Matthew 12:8, 11-13; Luke 6:6-11; John 5:1-17

24
MIRACLE SEEKERS
Summer, A.D. 28

Meanwhile Jesus and His disciples withdrew to the beach, followed by a huge crowd from all over Galilee, Judea, Jerusalem, Idumea, from beyond the Jordan River and even from as far away as Tyre and Sidon. For the news about His miracles had spread far and wide and vast numbers came to see Him for themselves.

He instructed His disciples to bring around a boat and have it standing ready to rescue Him in case He was crowded off the beach. For He had healed many that day, and as a result, great numbers of sick people were crowding around Him, trying to touch Him.

From Mark 3:7-10

Soon afterwards Jesus went out into the mountains to pray, and prayed all night. At daybreak He called together His followers and chose twelve of them to be the inner circle of His disciples. They were appointed as His "apostles," or "missionaries." Here are their names:
Simon, also called Peter,
Andrew, Simon's brother,
James,
John,
Philip,
Bartholomew,
Matthew,
Thomas,
James, the son of Alphaeus,
Simon, also called "Zealotes,"
Judas, son of James,
Judas Iscariot, who later betrayed Him.

From Luke 6:12-16

25
THE INNER CIRCLE

26
WAYS OF HAPPINESS AND LOVE

One day as the crowds were gathering, Jesus went up the hillside with His disciples, and sat down and taught them there.

"Humble men are very fortunate!" He told them, "for the Kingdom of Heaven is given to them!

"Those who mourn are fortunate! For they shall be comforted!

"The meek and lowly are fortunate! For the whole wide world belongs to them!

"Happy are those who long for justice, for they shall surely have it.

"Happy are the kind and merciful, for they shall be shown mercy.

"Happy are those whose hearts are pure, for they shall see God!

"Happy are those who strive for peace—they shall be called the sons of God!

"Happy are those who are persecuted because they are good, for the Kingdom of Heaven is theirs! When you are reviled and persecuted and lied about because you are My followers—wonderful!

"Be happy about it! Be very glad! for a tremendous reward awaits you up in heaven! And remember, the ancient prophets were persecuted too!

"Don't store up your profits here on earth, where they erode away, and can be stolen! But store them in heaven, where they never lose their value and are safe from thieves! If your profits are in heaven your heart will be there too!

"But, oh, the sorrows that await the rich! For they have had their happiness down here. They are fat and prosperous now, but a time of awful hunger is before them. Their careless laughter now means sorrow then.

"You cannot serve two masters: God and money. For you will hate one and love the other, or else the other way around.

"Listen, all of you! Love your enemies! Do good to those who hate you! Pray for the happiness of those who curse you; implore God's blessing on those who hurt you. If someone slaps you on one cheek, let him slap the other too! If someone demands your coat, give him your shirt besides! Give what you have to anyone who asks you for it; and when things are taken away from you, don't worry about getting them back. Treat others as you want them to treat you. Do you think you deserve credit for merely loving those who love you? Even the godless do that!

"Do for others what you want them to do for you. This is the teaching of the Old Testament in a nutshell."

From Matthew 5:1-12; 6:19-21, 24; 7:12; Luke 6:24, 25, 27-32

27 WAYS FOR WORRIERS

"Don't worry about things—food, drink, and clothes. For you already have life and a body—and they are far more important than what to eat and wear. Look at the birds! They don't worry about what to eat—they don't sow or reap or store up food—and your heavenly Father feeds them. And you are far more valuable to Him than they are! Will all your worries add a single moment to your life?

"And why worry about your clothes? Look at the field lilies! They don't worry about theirs! Yet King Solomon in all his glory was not clothed as beautifully as they! And if God cares so wonderfully for flowers that are here today and gone tomorrow, won't He more surely care for you, O men of little faith? So don't worry at all about having enough food and clothing.

"Don't be like the heathen! They take pride in these things and are deeply concerned about them. But your heavenly Father already knows perfectly well that you need them. And He will give them to you gladly if you put Him first in your life. So don't be anxious about tomorrow! God will take care of your tomorrow too! Live one day at a time."

From Matthew 6:25-34

28 WAYS OF PRAYER

"And now about prayer. When you pray, don't be like the hypocrites who pretend piety by praying publicly on street corners and in the synagogues where everyone can see them! Truly, that is all the reward they will ever get! But when you pray, go away by yourself, all alone, and shut the door behind you and pray to your Father secretly, and your Father, who knows your secrets, will reward you. Don't recite the same prayer over and over, as the heathen do, who think prayers are answered only by repeating them again and again. Remember, your Father knows exactly what you need even before you ask Him!

"Ask, and you will be given what you ask for! Seek, and you will find! Knock, and the door will be opened! For everyone who asks receives. Anyone who seeks finds. If only you will knock, the door will open.

"Pray along these lines: 'Our Father in heaven, we honor Your holy name. We ask that Your kingdom will come soon. May Your will be done here on earth, just as it is in heaven. Give us our food again today, as usual, and forgive us our sins, just as we have forgiven those who have sinned against us. Don't bring us into temptation, but deliver us from the Evil One. For Yours is the kingdom and the power and the glory forever. Amen.' "

From Matthew 6:5-13; 7:7, 8

29
AMAZING FAITH

When Jesus arrived in Capernaum, a Roman army captain came and pled with Him to come to his home and heal his servant boy who was in bed paralyzed and racked with pain. Some respected Jewish elders began pleading earnestly with Jesus to come with them and help the man. They told Him what a wonderful person the captain was. "If anyone deserves Your help, it is he," they said, "for he loves the Jews and even paid personally for building us a synagogue!"

"Yes," Jesus said, "I will come and heal him."

Then the officer said, "Sir, I am not worthy to have You in my home; and it isn't necessary for You to come. If right here You will just say, 'Be healed,' my servant will get well! I know, because I am under the authority of my superior officers, and I have authority over my soldiers, and I say to one, 'Go,' and he goes, and to another 'Come,' and he comes, and to my slave boy, 'Do this or that,' and he does it. And I know You have authority to tell his sickness to go—and it will go!"

Jesus stood there amazed! Turning to the crowd following Him, He said, "I haven't seen faith like this in all the land of Israel! And I tell you this, that many Gentiles like this Roman officer shall come from all over the world and sit down in the Kingdom of Heaven with Abraham, Isaac, and Jacob. And many an Israelite—those for whom the kingdom was prepared—shall be cast into outer darkness, to the place of weeping and torment."

Then Jesus said to the Roman officer, "Go on home. What you have believed has happened!" And the boy was healed that same hour!

From Matthew 8:5-13; Luke 7:3-5

30
BIG QUESTION

Not long afterwards Jesus went with His disciples to the village of Nain, with the usual vast crowd at His heels. As He approached the village gate, a funeral procession was coming out. The boy who had died was the only son of his widowed mother, and following along with her were many mourners from the village.

When the Lord saw her, His heart overflowed with sympathy. "Don't cry!" He said. Then, as He walked over to the coffin and touched it, the bearers stopped. And He said, "Laddie, come back to life again!" The boy sat up and began to talk to those around him! And Jesus gave him back to his mother.

Then a great fear swept the crowd, and they exclaimed with praises to God, "A mighty prophet has risen among us," and, "We have seen the hand of God at work today." The report of what He did that morning raced from end to end of Judea and out across the borders into the surrounding country.

The disciples of John the Baptist soon heard of all that Jesus was doing. When they told John about it, he sent two of his disciples to Jesus to ask Him, "Are You really the Messiah? Or shall we keep on looking for Him?"

The two disciples found Jesus while He was curing many sick people of their various diseases, healing the lame and the blind and casting out evil spirits. So they asked Him John's question.

Jesus told them, "Go back to John and tell him about the miracles you've seen Me do—The blind people I've healed, and the lame people now walking without help, and the cured lepers, and the deaf who hear, and the dead raised to life; and tell him about My preaching the Good News to the poor. Then give him this message, 'Blessed are those who don't doubt Me.' "

From Matthew 11:4-6; Luke 7:11-21

31
MUCH FORGIVEN, MUCH LOVED

One of the Pharisees asked Jesus to come to his home for lunch, and Jesus accepted the invitation. As they sat down to eat, a woman of the streets, who had heard He was there, brought an exquisite flask filled with expensive perfume, and going in, she knelt behind Him at His feet, weeping until His feet were wet with her tears; and she wiped them off with her hair and kissed them and poured the perfume on them.

When Jesus' host, a Pharisee, saw what was happening and who the woman was, he said to himself, "This proves that Jesus is no prophet, for if God had really sent Him, He would know what kind of woman this one is!"

Then Jesus spoke up and answered his thoughts! "Simon," He said to the Pharisee, "I have something to say to you."

"All right, Teacher," Simon replied, "go ahead."

Then Jesus told him this story: "A man loaned money to two people—$5,000 to one and $500 to the other. But neither of them could pay him back, so he kindly forgave them both, letting them keep the money! Which do you suppose loved him most after that?"

"I suppose the one who owed him the most," answered Simon.

"Correct," Jesus agreed. Then He turned toward the woman and said to Simon, "Look! See this woman kneeling here! When I entered your home, you didn't bother to offer Me water to wash the dust from My feet, but she has washed them with her tears and wiped them with her hair! You refused Me the customary kiss of greeting, but she has kissed My feet again and again from the time I first came in. You neglected the usual courtesy of olive oil to anoint My head, but she has covered My feet with rare perfume. Therefore her sins —and they are many—are forgiven, for she loved Me much; but one who is forgiven little shows little love!"

And He said to her, "Your sins are forgiven!"

Then the other men at the table said to themselves, "Who does this man think He is, going around forgiving sins?"

And Jesus said to the woman, "Your faith has saved you; go in peace."

From Luke 7:36-50

32
LISTEN! HEAR!

Not long afterward, Jesus left the house where He was staying and went down to the shore, where an immense crowd soon gathered. He got into a boat and taught from it as the people listened on the beach. He used many illustrations in His sermon, such as this one:

"A farmer was sowing grain in his fields. As he scattered the seed across the ground, some fell beside a path, and the birds came and ate it. And some fell on rocky soil where there was little depth of earth; the plants sprang up quickly enough in the shallow soil, but the hot sun soon scorched them and they withered and died, for they had so little root. Other seeds fell among thorns, and the thorns choked out the tender blades. But some fell on good soil and produced a crop that was 30, 60 and even 100 times as much as had been planted.

"If you have ears, listen!

"Now here is the explanation of the illustration I used about the farmer planting grain: The hard path where some seed fell represents the heart of a person who hears the good news about the kingdom and doesn't understand it; then Satan comes and snatches away the seeds from his heart.

"The shallow, rocky soil represents the heart of a man who hears the message and receives it with real joy, but he doesn't have much depth in his life, and the seeds don't root very deeply, and after a while when troubles come, or persecution begins because of his convictions, his enthusiasm fades, and he drops out.

"The ground covered with thistles represents a man who hears the message, but the cares of this life and his longing for riches choke out God's words, and he becomes unfruitful.

"The good ground represents the heart of a man who listens to the message and understands it and produces a crop many times larger than the original seed—30, 60 or even 100 times as much."

When Jesus had finished these illustrations, He returned to His home town, Nazareth in Galilee, and taught there in the synagogue and astonished everyone with His wisdom and His miracles!

From Matthew 13:1-9, 18-23, 53, 54

33
FROM PANIC TO PEACE

[One] evening Jesus said to His disciples, "Let's cross to the other side of the lake." So they took Him just as He was and started out, leaving the crowds behind (though other boats followed along). Soon a terrible storm arose. High waves began to break into the boat until it was nearly full of water and about to sink.

Jesus was asleep at the back of the boat with His head on a cushion. Frantically they wakened Him, shouting, "Lord, save us! We're sinking! Don't You even care that we are all about to drown?"

Then He rebuked the wind and said to the sea, "Quiet down!" And the wind fell, and there was a great calm!

And He asked them, "Why were you so fearful? Don't you even yet have confidence in Me?"

And they were filled with awe and said among themselves, "Who is this man, that even the winds and seas obey Him?"

From Matthew 8:25; Mark 4:35-41

34
DESPERATE

When Jesus had gone across by boat to the other side of the lake, the crowds received Him with open arms, for they had been waiting for Him.

And now a man named Jairus, a leader of a Jewish synagogue, came and fell down at Jesus' feet and began to beg Him to come to his home, for his only child, a little girl twelve years old, was dying. Jesus went with him, pushing through the crowds.

As they went, a woman came up behind and touched Him for healing, for she had been slowly bleeding for twelve years, and could find no cure (though she had spent everything she had on doctors). But the instant she touched the edge of His robe, the bleeding stopped.

"Who touched Me?" Jesus asked.

Everyone denied it, and Peter said, "Master, so many are crowding against You—"

But Jesus said, "No, it was someone who deliberately touched Me, for I felt healing power go out from Me." When the woman realized that Jesus knew, she began to tremble and fell down before Him and told why she had touched Him and that she was now well.

He said to her, "Daughter, your faith has healed you! Go in peace."

While He was still talking with her, a messenger arrived from the Jairus home with the news that his little girl was dead. "She's gone," they told her father; "there is no use troubling the Teacher now."

But Jesus ignored their comments and said to Jairus, "Don't be afraid. Just trust Me." Then Jesus halted the crowd and wouldn't let anyone go on with Him to Jairus' home except Peter and James and John.

When they arrived, Jesus saw that all was in great confusion, with unrestrained weeping and wailing. He went inside and spoke to the people. "Why all this weeping and commotion?" He asked. "The child isn't dead; she is only asleep!"

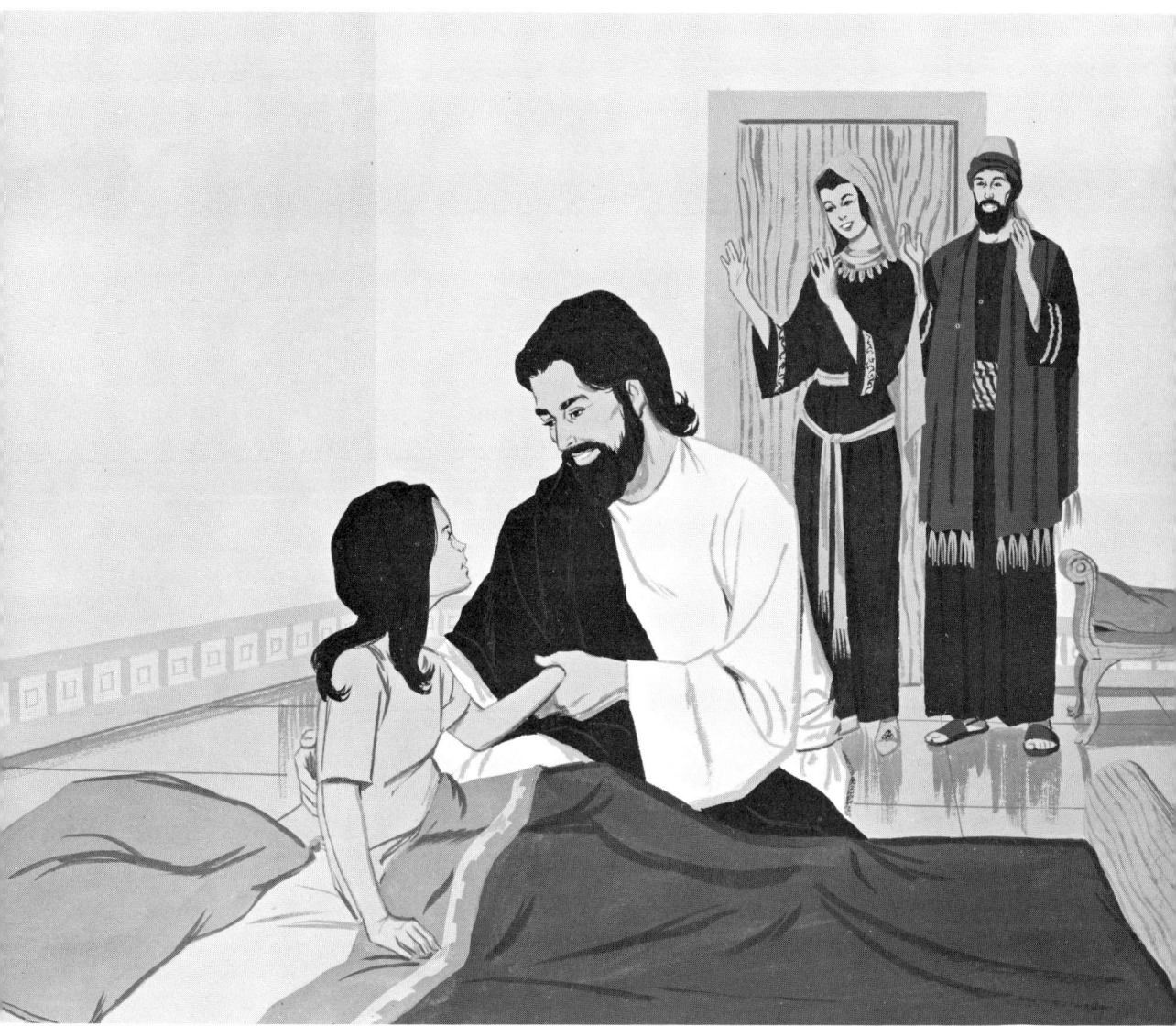

This brought scoffing and laughter, for they all knew she was dead. But He told them all to leave, and taking the little girl's father and mother and His three disciples, He went into the room where she was lying. Taking her by the hand, He said to her, "Get up, little girl!" And she jumped up and walked around!

Her parents were overcome with happiness, but Jesus insisted that they not tell anyone the details of what had happened. [But] the report of this wonderful miracle swept the entire countryside.

From Matthew 9:26; Mark 5:21, 36-42; Luke 8:40-49, 53, 56

35
BIRTHDAY PARTY MURDER
Early A.D. 29

Some months earlier Herod had arrested John and chained him in prison at the demand of Herodias, his brother Philip's ex-wife, because John had told Herod it was wrong for him to marry her. King Herod would have killed John but was afraid of a riot, for all the people believed John was a prophet. But at a birthday party for Herod, Herodias' daughter came in and danced before them and greatly pleased them all. "Ask me for anything you like," the king vowed, "even half of my kingdom, and I will give it to you!"

She went out and consulted her mother, who told her, "Ask for John the Baptist's head!" So the girl hurried back to the king and announced, "I want the head of John the Baptist—right now—on a tray!"

Then the king was sorry, but he was embarrassed to break his oath in front of his guests.

So John was beheaded in the prison. His head was brought in on a tray and given to the girl, who took it to her mother.

Then John's disciples came for his body and buried it, and went and told Jesus. As soon as Jesus heard what

had happened, He went off by Himself in a boat to a remote area.

About that time King Herod heard about the wonderful miracles that Jesus was doing. And Herod said to his men, "This must be John the Baptist, come back to life again. That is why He can do these miracles."

From Matthew 14:1-6, 10-13; Mark 6:22-26

36 MORE THAN ENOUGH

The apostles now returned to Jesus from their tour and told Him all they had done and what they had said to the people they visited.

Then Jesus told them, "Let's get away from the crowds for awhile and rest." For so many people were coming and going that they scarcely had time to eat! And they left by boat for a quieter spot. But many people saw them leaving and recognized them and ran on ahead along the shore and met them as they landed! So the usual vast crowd was there as He stepped from the boat; and He had pity on them because they were like sheep without a shepherd. And He taught them many things they needed to know.

Late in the afternoon His disciples came to Him and said, "Tell them to go away to the nearby villages and farms and buy themselves some food, for there is nothing to eat here in this desolate spot and it is getting late."

But Jesus said, "You feed them!"

"With what?" they asked. "It would take a fortune to buy food for all this crowd!"

"How much food do we have?" He asked.

Then Andrew, Simon Peter's brother, spoke up. "There's a youngster here with five barley loaves and a couple of fish! But what good is that with all this mob?"

"Tell everyone to sit down," Jesus ordered. And all 5,000 of them (that was the approximate count of the men only) sat down on the grassy slopes in groups of 50 or 100. Then Jesus took the loaves and gave thanks to God and passed them out to the people. Afterwards He did the same with the fish. And everyone had all he wanted.

"Now gather the scraps," Jesus told His disciples, "so that nothing is wasted." And 12 baskets were filled with the leftovers!

When the people realized what a great miracle had happened, they exclaimed, "Surely, He is the Prophet we have been expecting!"

From Mark 6:30-38, 40; John 6:8-14

Immediately after this Jesus told His disciples to get into their boat and cross to the other side of the lake, while He stayed to get the people started home. After sending them away, He went into the hills alone to pray.

Night fell, and out on the lake the disciples were in trouble. For the wind had risen and they were fighting heavy seas. About four o'clock in the morning when they were three or four miles out Jesus came to them, walking on the water! The disciples screamed in terror when they saw Him for they thought He was a ghost. But Jesus immediately spoke to them and reassured them, telling them not to be afraid!

Then Peter said, "Sir, if it is really You, tell me to come over to You, walking on the water!"

"Yes," the Lord said, "Come!" So Peter went over the side of the boat and walked on the water toward Jesus!

But when Peter looked around at the high waves, he was terrified and began to sink! "Save me, Lord!" he shouted.

Instantly Jesus reached out His hand and rescued him. "O man of little faith," Jesus said, "Why did you doubt?" And when they had climbed into the boat, the wind stopped.

The others sat there, awestruck. "You really are the Son of God," they said.

From Matthew 14:22-33; John 6:19

37
RESCUE AT DAWN

38
PEOPLE, PEOPLE, PEOPLE!
Early Summer, A.D. 29

Jesus returned one day to the Sea of Galilee and went up onto a hill and sat down. And a large crowd brought Him their lame, blind, maimed, and those who couldn't speak, and many others, and laid them before Jesus, and He healed them all. What a spectacle it was! Those who hadn't been able to say a word before were talking excitedly, and those with missing arms and legs had new ones; the crippled were walking and jumping around, and those who had been blind were gazing about them! The crowds just marveled, and praised the God of Israel!

A deaf man with a speech impediment was brought to Him, and they begged Jesus to lay His hands on the man and heal him. Jesus led him away from the crowd and put His fingers into the man's ears, then spat and touched the man's tongue with the spittle. And looking up to heaven He sighed and commanded, "Open!" Instantly the man could hear perfectly and speak plainly!

Jesus told the crowd not to spread the news, but the more He forbade them, the more they made it known, for they were overcome with utter amazement. Again and again they said, "Everything He does is wonderful; He even corrects deafness and stammering!"

From Matthew 15:29-31; Mark 7:32-37

One day about this time as another great crowd gathered, the people ran out of food. Jesus called His disciples and said, "I pity them; for they have been here three days and have nothing to eat. If I send them home

39

EXTRAORDINARY PICNIC

without feeding them, they will faint along on the road! For some of them have come a long distance."

His disciples said, "Are we supposed to find food for them here in the desert?"

"How many loaves of bread do you have?" He asked, and they replied, "Seven."

So He told the crowd to sit down on the ground. Then He took the seven loaves, thanked God, broke them into pieces and passed them to His disciples; and the disciples placed them before the people. They found a few small fish too, which Jesus also blessed and told the disciples to serve. And the whole crowd ate until they were full, and afterwards He sent them home. There were about 4,000 people in the crowd that day and when the scraps were picked up after the meal, there were seven very large basketfuls of them!

From Mark 8:1-9

40
THE TOUCH THAT HEALS
Midsummer, A.D. 29

Another day, when Jesus arrived at the town of Bethsaida, some people brought a blind man to Him and begged Him to touch and heal him. Jesus took the blind man by the hand and led him out of the village, and spat upon his eyes, and laid His hands over them. "Can you see anything now?" Jesus asked him.

The man looked around. "Yes!" he said, "I see men! But I can't see them very clearly; they look like tree trunks walking around!"

Then Jesus placed His hands over the man's eyes again and as he looked intently, his sight was completely restored, and he saw everything clearly, drinking in the sights around him. Jesus sent him home to his family. "Don't even go back to the village first," He said.

From Mark 8:22-26

One day Jesus asked His disciples, "Who are the people saying I am?"

"Well," they replied, "some say John the Baptist; some, Elijah; some, Jeremiah or one of the other prophets."

Then He asked them, "Who do *you* think I am?"

Simon Peter answered, "The Christ, the Messiah, the Son of the living God."

"God has blessed you, Simon, son of Jonah," Jesus said, "for My Father in heaven has personally revealed this to you—this is not from any human source." Then He warned the disciples against telling others that He was the Messiah.

From then on Jesus began to speak plainly to His disciples about going to Jerusalem, and of what would happen to Him there—that He would suffer at the hands of the Jewish leaders, that He would be killed, and that three days later He would be raised to life again.

Six days later Jesus took Peter, James and his brother John to the top of a high and lonely hill, and as they watched, His appearance changed so that His face shone like the sun and His clothing became dazzling white. Far more glorious than any earthly process could ever make it! Suddenly Moses and Elijah appeared and were talking with Him! They were splendid in appearance, glorious to see; and they were speaking of His death at Jerusalem, to be carried out in accordance with God's plan.

Peter and the others had been very drowsy and had fallen asleep. Now they woke up and saw Jesus covered with brightness and glory, and the two men standing with Him.

Peter blurted out, "Lord, it's wonderful that we can be here! If You want me to, I'll make three shelters, one for You and one for Moses and one for Elijah!" He said this just to be talking, for he didn't know what else to

41

SWORN TO SECRECY

say and they were all scared stiff. But even as Peter said it, a bright cloud came over them, and a voice from the cloud said, "This is My beloved Son, and I am wonderfully pleased with Him. Listen to Him. Obey Him."

At this the disciples fell on their faces, terribly frightened. Jesus came over and touched them. "Get up; don't be afraid," He said. And when they looked, only Jesus was with them.

As they were going down the mountain, Jesus commanded them not to tell anyone what they had seen until after He had risen from the dead. So they kept it to themselves, but often talked about it, and wondered what He meant by "rising from the dead."

His disciples asked, "Why do the Jewish leaders insist Elijah must return before the Messiah comes?"

Jesus replied, "They are right. Elijah must come and set everything in order. And, in fact, he has already come, but he wasn't recognized and was badly mistreated. And I, the Son of Man, shall also suffer at their hands." Then the disciples realized He was speaking of John the Baptist.

From Matthew 16:14-17, 20, 21; 17:1-13; Mark 9:3, 6, 7, 10; Luke 9:18, 31, 32

42
TIME FOR TEACHING AND TAXES
Late Summer, A.D. 29

Leaving that region they traveled through Galilee where Jesus tried to avoid all publicity, so that He could spend time with His disciples, teaching them. He would say to them, "I, the Son of Man, am going to be betrayed and killed and three days later I will return to life again."

But they didn't understand and were afraid to ask Him what He meant.

On their arrival in Capernaum, the Temple tax collectors came to Peter and asked him, "Doesn't your Master pay taxes?"

"Sure He does," Peter replied.

Then he went into the house to talk to Jesus about it, but before he had a chance to speak, Jesus asked him, "What do you think, Peter? Do kings levy assessments against their own people, or against conquered foreigners?"

"Against the foreigners," Peter replied.

"Well, then," Jesus said, "the citizens are free! However, we don't want to offend the Temple tax collectors, so go down to the shore and throw in a line. Open the mouth of the first fish you catch. You will find a coin to cover the taxes for both of us, then go and pay them."

From Matthew 17:24-26; Mark 9:30-32

43 SEVENTY TIMES SEVEN

Then Peter came to Jesus and asked, "Sir, how often should I forgive a brother who sins against me? Seven times?"

"No!" Jesus replied, "seventy times seven! The Kingdom of Heaven can be compared to a king who decided to bring his accounts up to date. In the process, one of his debtors was brought in who owed him $10,000,000! He couldn't pay, so the king ordered him sold for the debt, also his wife and children and everything he had.

"But the man fell down before the king, his face in the dust, and said, 'Oh, Sir, be patient with me and I will repay it all.' Then the king was filled with pity for him and released him and forgave his debt!

"But when the man left the king, he went to a man who owed him $2,000 and grabbed him by the throat and demanded instant payment. The man fell down before him and begged him to give him a little time. 'Be patient and I will pay it,' he pled. But his creditor wouldn't wait. He had the man arrested and jailed until the debt would be paid in full.

"Then the man's friends went to the king and told him what had happened. And the king called before him the man he had forgiven and said, 'You evil-hearted wretch! Here I forgave you all that tremendous debt you owed me, just because you asked me to—shouldn't you have mercy on others, just as I had mercy on you?' Then the angry king sent the man to the torture chamber until he had paid every last penny due. So shall My heavenly Father do to you if you refuse to truly forgive your brothers."

From Matthew 18:21-35

44 MANY OPINIONS

When the crowds in the Temple heard Jesus, some of them declared, "This man surely is the prophet who will come just before the Messiah." Others said, "He *is* the Messiah." Still others, "But He can't be! Will the Messiah come from Galilee? For the Scriptures clearly state that the Messiah will be born of the royal line of David, in Bethlehem, the village where David was born." So the crowd was divided about Him. And some wanted Him arrested, but no one touched Him.

The Temple police who had been sent to arrest Him

returned to the chief priests and Pharisees. "Why didn't you bring Him in?" they demanded.

"He says such wonderful things!" the police mumbled. "We've never heard anything like it."

"So you also have been led astray?" the Pharisees mocked. "Is there a single one of us Jewish rulers or Pharisees who believes He is the Messiah? These stupid crowds do, yes; but what do they know about it? A curse upon them anyway!"

Then Nicodemus spoke up. (Remember him? He was the Jewish leader who came secretly to interview Jesus at night.) "Is it legal to convict a man before he is even tried?" he asked.

They replied, "Are you a wretched Galilean too? Search the Scriptures and see for yourself—no prophets will come from Galilee!"

The meeting broke up and everybody went home. Jesus returned to the Mount of Olives.

From John 7:40-53; 8:1

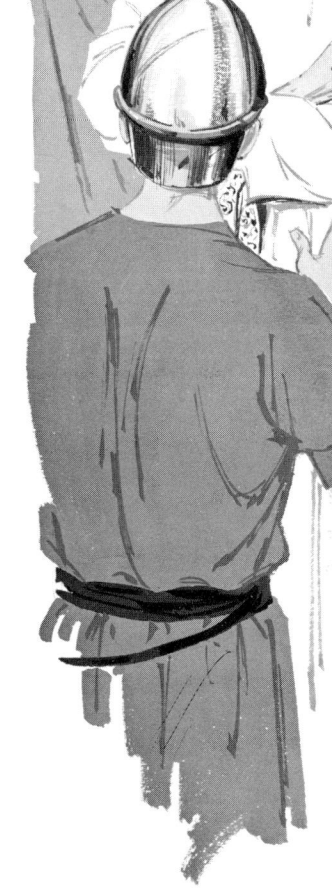

As Jesus was walking along, He saw a man blind from birth.

"Master," His disciples asked Him, "why was this man born blind? Was it a result of his own sins or those of his parents?"

"Neither," Jesus answered. "But to demonstrate the power of God."

Then He spat on the ground and made mud from the spittle and smoothed the mud over the blind man's eyes, and told him, "Go and wash in the Pool of Siloam" (the word "Siloam" means "Sent"). So the man went where

45

SEEING IS BELIEVING

he was sent and washed and came back seeing!

His neighbors and others who knew him as a blind beggar asked each other, "Is this the same fellow—that beggar?" Some said yes, and some said no. "It can't be the same man," they thought, "but he surely looks like him!"

And the beggar said, "I *am* the same man!"

Then they asked him how in the world he could see. What had happened? And he told them, "A man they call Jesus made mud and smoothed it over my eyes and told me to go to the Pool of Siloam and wash off the mud. I did, and I can see!"

"Where is He now?" they asked.

"I don't know," he replied.

Then they took the man to the Pharisees. (Now as it happened, this all occurred on a Sabbath.) The Pharisees asked him all about it. So he told them how Jesus had smoothed the mud over his eyes, and when it was washed away, he could see!

Some of them said, "Then this fellow Jesus is not from God, because He is working on the Sabbath!"

Others said, "But how could an ordinary sinner do such miracles?" So there was a deep division of opinion among them.

Then the Pharisees turned on the man who had been blind and demanded, "This man who opened your eyes —who do you say He is?"

"I think He must be a prophet sent from God," the man replied.

The Jewish leaders wouldn't believe he had been blind, until they called in his parents and asked them, "Is this your son? Was he born blind? If so, how can he see?"

His parents replied, "We know this is our son and that he was born blind, but we don't know what happened to make him see, or who did it. He is old enough to speak for himself. Ask him!" They said this in fear of the Jewish leaders who had announced that anyone saying Jesus was the Messiah would be excommunicated.

So for the second time they called in the man who had been blind and told him, "Give the glory to God, not to Jesus, for we know Jesus is an evil person."

"I don't know whether He is good or bad," the man replied, "but I know this: *I was blind, and now I see!*"

"But what did He do?" they asked. "How did He heal you?"

"Look!" the man exclaimed. "I told you once; didn't you listen? Do you want to hear it again? Do you want to become His disciples too?"

Then they cursed him and said, "You are His disciple, but we are disciples of Moses. We know God has spoken to Moses, but as for this fellow, we don't know anything about Him."

"That's very strange!" the man replied. "He can heal blind men, but you don't know anything about Him! Well, God doesn't listen to evil men, but He has opened ears to those who worship Him and do His will. Since the world began, there has never been anyone who could open the eyes of someone born blind. If this man were not from God, He couldn't do it."

"You illegitimate bastard, you!" they shouted.

"Are you trying to teach *us*?" And they threw him out.

When Jesus heard what had happened, He found the man and said, "Do you believe in the Messiah?"

The man answered, "Who is He, Sir, for I want to."

"You have seen Him," Jesus said, "and He is speaking to you!"

"Yes, Lord," the man said, "I believe!" and he worshiped Jesus.

Then Jesus told him, "I have come into the world to give sight to those who are spiritually blind and to show those who think they see that they are blind."

From John 9:1-3, 6-39

46
ALL FOR HIS OWN

"Anyone refusing to walk through the gate into a sheepfold, but sneaks over the wall instead, must surely be a thief! For a shepherd comes through the gate! The gatekeeper opens the gate for him, and the sheep hear his voice and come to him; and he calls his own sheep by name and leads them out. He walks ahead of them; and they follow him, for they recognize his voice. They won't follow a stranger, but will run from him, for they don't recognize his voice."

Those who heard Jesus use this illustration didn't understand what He meant, so He explained it to them. "I am the Gate for the sheep," He said. "All others who came before Me are thieves and robbers. But the true sheep did not listen to them. Yes, I am the Gate. Those who come in by way of the Gate will be saved and will go in and out and find green pastures. The thief's purpose is to steal, kill and destroy. My purpose is to give eternal life—abundantly!

"I am the Good Shepherd. The Good Shepherd lays down His life for the sheep. A hired man will run when he sees a wolf coming, and leave the sheep, for they aren't his and he isn't their shepherd. And so the wolf leaps on them and scatters the flock. The hired man runs because he is hired and has no real concern for the sheep.

"I am the Good Shepherd and know My own sheep, and they know Me, just as My Father knows Me and I know the Father; and I lay down My life for the sheep.

No one can kill Me without My consent—I lay down My life voluntarily. For I have the right and power to lay it down when I want to and also the right and power to take it again. For the Father has given Me this right."

When He said these things, the Jewish leaders were again divided in their opinions about Him.

From John 10:1-15, 18, 19

47
WHICH NEIGHBORS?

One day an expert on Moses' laws came to Jesus asking this question: "Teacher, what does a man need to do to live forever in heaven?"

Jesus replied, "What does Moses' law say about it?"

"It says," he replied, "that you must love the Lord your God with all your heart, and with all your soul, and with all your strength, and with all your mind. And you must love your neighbor just as much as you love yourself."

"Right!" Jesus told him. "Do this and you shall live!" The man wanted to justify his lack of love for some kinds of people, so he asked, "Which neighbors?"

Jesus replied with an illustration: "A Jew going on a trip from Jerusalem to Jericho was attacked by bandits. They stripped him of his clothes and money and beat him up and left him lying half dead beside the road. By chance a Jewish priest came along; and though he saw the man lying there, he crossed to the other side of the road and went by. A Jewish Temple-assistant did the same thing; he, too, left him lying there.

"But a despised Samaritan came along; and when he

saw him, he felt deep pity for him. Kneeling beside him, the Samaritan soothed his wounds with medicine and bandaged them.

"Then he put the man on his donkey and walked along beside him till they came to an inn. He nursed him through the night. The next day he handed the innkeeper two twenty-dollar bills and told him to take care of the man. 'If his bill runs higher than that,' he said, 'I'll pay the difference the next time I am here.'

"Now which of these three would you say was a neighbor to the bandits' victim?"

The man replied, "The one who showed him some pity."

Then Jesus said, "Yes, now go and do the same."

From Luke 10:25-37

As Jesus and the disciples continued on their way to the City of Jerusalem, they came to a village where a woman named Martha welcomed them into her home. Her sister Mary sat spellbound on the floor, listening to Jesus as He talked.

Martha was the jittery type and was worrying over the big dinner she was preparing. She came to Jesus and said, "Sir, doesn't it seem unfair to You that my sister just sits there while I do all the work? Make her come and help me."

But the Lord said to her, "Martha, dear friend, you are so upset over all these details! There is really only one thing worth your concern. Mary has chosen it—and I won't take it away from her!"

From Luke 10:38-42

48
UPSET OVER DETAILS

49
PROOF ENOUGH
December, A.D. 29

One Sabbath as Jesus was teaching in a synagogue, He saw a seriously handicapped woman who had been bent double for 18 years and was unable to straighten herself and stand upright. Calling her over to Him, Jesus said, "Woman, you are healed of your sickness!" He touched her, and instantly she could stand straight! How she praised and thanked God!

But the local Jewish leader in charge of the synagogue was very angry about it because Jesus had healed

her on the Sabbath day. "There are six days of the week to work," the leader shouted to the crowd. "Those are the days to come for healing, not on the Sabbath!"

But the Lord replied, "You hypocrites! You work on the Sabbath! Don't you untie your cattle from their stalls on the Sabbath and lead them out for water? And is it wrong for Me, just because it is the Sabbath day, to free this Jewish woman from Satan's 18 years of bondage?"

This shamed His enemies. But the rest of the people rejoiced at the wonderful things He did.

It was winter, and Jesus was in Jerusalem at the time of the Dedication Celebration. He was at the Temple, walking through the section known as Solomon's Cloister.

The Jewish leaders surrounded Him and asked, "How long are you going to keep us in suspense? If You are the Messiah, tell us plainly."

"I have already told you, and you didn't believe Me," Jesus replied. "The proof is in the miracles I do in the name of My Father."

Then again the Jewish leaders picked up stones to kill Him.

Jesus said, "At God's direction I have done many a miracle to help the people. For which one are you killing Me?"

They replied, "Not for any good work, but for blasphemy. You, a mere man, have declared Yourself to be God."

"In your own Law it says that men are gods!" He replied, "So if the Scripture—which cannot be untrue—speaks of those as gods, to whom the message of God came, do you call it blasphemy when the one sanctified and sent into the world by the Father says, 'I am the Son of God'?"

From Luke 13:10-17; John 10:22-25, 31-36

50 FOUND!

Dishonest tax collectors and other notorious sinners were all gathering to listen to Jesus' sermons; and the Jewish religious leaders and the experts on Jewish law complained because He was associating with such people—even eating with them!

So Jesus used this illustration: "If you had 100 sheep and one of them strayed away and was lost in the wilderness, wouldn't you leave the 99 others to go and search for the lost one until you found it? And then you would joyfully carry it home on your shoulders. When you arrived you would call together your friends and neighbors to rejoice with you because your lost sheep was found. Well, in the same way heaven will be happier over the one lost sinner who returns to God than over the 99 others who haven't strayed away!"

To further illustrate the point, He told them this story: "A man had two sons. When the younger told his father, 'I want my share of your estate now, instead of waiting until you die!' his father agreed to divide his wealth between his sons.

"A few days later this younger son packed all his belongings and took a trip to a distant land, and there wasted all his money on parties and prostitutes. About the time his money was gone, a great famine swept over the land, and he began to starve. He persuaded a local farmer to hire him, and the farmer sent him out into the fields to feed pigs. But even so, the boy became so hungry he gladly would have eaten the pods he was feeding the swine. And no one gave him anything.

"When he finally came to his senses, he said to himself, 'At home even the hired men have food enough and

to spare, and here I am, dying of hunger! I will go home to my father and say, "Father, I have sinned against both heaven and you and am no longer worthy of being called your son. Please take me on as a hired man."'

"So he returned home to his father. And while he was still a long distance away, his father saw him coming and was filled with loving pity and ran and embraced him and kissed him.

"The son said to him, 'Father, I have sinned against heaven and you and am not worthy of being called your son.' But his father said to the slaves, 'Quick! Bring the finest robe in the house and put it on him. And a jeweled ring for his finger; and shoes! And kill the calf we have in the fattening pen. We must celebrate with a feast, for this son of mine was dead and has returned to life! He was lost and is found!' So the party began.

"Meanwhile the older son was in the fields working; when he returned home, he heard music coming from the house. He asked one of the servants what was going on. 'Your brother is back,' he was told, 'and your father has killed the calf we were fattening and has prepared a great feast to celebrate his coming home again unharmed.'

"The older brother was angry and wouldn't go in. His father came out and begged him, but he replied, 'All these years I've worked hard for you and never once refused to do a single thing you told me to; and in all that time you never gave me even one young goat for a feast with my friends. Yet when this son of yours comes back after spending your money, you celebrate by killing the finest calf we have on the place.'

"'Look, my dear son,' his father said to him, 'you and I are very close, and everything I have is yours. But it is right to celebrate. For he is your brother; and he was dead and has come back to life! He was lost and is found!'"

From Luke 15:1-7, 10-32

51

MORE THAN ENOUGH PROOF

February, A.D. 30

Do you remember Mary, who poured the costly perfume on Jesus' feet and wiped them with her hair? Well, her brother Lazarus, who lived in Bethany with his sisters Mary and Martha, was sick. So the two sisters sent a message to Jesus telling Him, "Sir, your good friend is very, very sick."

But when Jesus heard about it, He said, "The purpose of his illness is not death, but for the glory of God. I, the Son of God, will receive glory from this situation." Although Jesus was very fond of Martha, Mary and Lazarus, He stayed where He was for the next two days and made no move to go to them.

Finally, after the two days, He said to His disciples, "Let's go to Judea."

But His disciples objected, "Master," they said, "only a few days ago the Jewish leaders in Judea were trying to kill You. Are You going there again?"

Then Jesus said, "Our friend Lazarus has gone to sleep, but now I will go and waken him!"

The disciples, thinking Jesus meant Lazarus was having a good night's rest, said, "That means he is getting better!" But Jesus meant Lazarus had died.

Then He told them plainly, "Lazarus is dead. And for your sake, I am glad I wasn't there, for this will give you another opportunity to believe in Me. Come, let's go to him."

When they arrived at Bethany, they were told that Lazarus had already been in his tomb for four days! Bethany was only a couple of miles down the road from Jerusalem and many of the Jewish leaders had come to pay their respects and to console Martha and Mary on their loss.

When Martha got word that Jesus was coming, she went to meet Him. But Mary stayed at home. Martha said to Jesus, "Sir, if You had been here, my brother wouldn't have died. And even now it's not too late, for I know that God will bring my brother back to life again, if You will only ask Him to."

Jesus told her, "Your brother will come back to life again."

"Yes," Martha said, "when everyone else does, on Resurrection Day."

Jesus told her, "I am the one who raises the dead and gives them life again. Anyone who believes in Me, even though he dies like anyone else, shall live again. He is given eternal life for believing in Me and shall never perish. Do you believe this, Martha?"

"Yes, Master," she told Him. "I believe You are the Messiah, the Son of God, the one we have so long awaited." Then she left Him and returned to Mary and calling her aside from the mourners told her, "He is here and wants to see you." Mary left immediately to go to Him.

Now Jesus had stayed outside the village, at the place where Martha met Him. When the Jewish leaders who were at the house trying to console Mary saw her hastily leave, they assumed she was going to Lazarus' tomb to weep; so they followed her. When Mary arrived where Jesus was, she fell down at His feet, saying, "Sir, if You had been here, my brother would still be alive."

When Jesus saw her weeping and the Jewish leaders wailing with her, He was moved with indignation and deeply troubled. "Where is he buried?" He asked them.

They told Him, "Come and see."

Tears came to Jesus' eyes. "They were close friends," the Jewish leaders said. "See how much He loved him."

But some said, "This fellow healed a blind man—why couldn't He keep Lazarus from dying?" And again Jesus was moved with deep anger. Then they came to the tomb. It was a cave with a heavy stone rolled across its door.

"Roll the stone aside," Jesus told them.

But Martha, the dead man's sister, said, "By now the smell will be terrible, for he has been dead four days."

"But didn't I tell you that you will see a wonderful miracle from God if you believe?" Jesus asked her.

So they rolled the stone aside. Then Jesus looked up to heaven and said, "Father, thank You for hearing Me. You always hear Me, of course, but I said it because of all these people standing here, so that they will believe You sent Me."

Then He shouted, "Lazarus, come out!" And Lazarus came—bound up in the gravecloth, his face muffled in a head swath. Jesus told them, "Unwrap him and let him go!"

And so at last many of the Jewish leaders who were with Mary and saw it happen finally believed on Him! But some went away to the Pharisees and reported it to them.

From John 11:1-8, 11-15, 17-46

The chief priests and Pharisees convened a council to discuss the situation. "What are we going to do?" they asked each other, "for this man certainly does miracles. If we let Him alone, the whole nation will follow Him— and then the Roman army will come and kill us and take over the Jewish government."

But one of them, Caiaphas, who was High Priest that year, said, "You stupid idiots—let this one man die for the people—why should the whole nation perish?"

This prophecy that Jesus should die for the entire nation came from Caiaphas in his position as High

52
DEATH PLOT

Priest—he didn't think of it by himself, but was inspired to say it. It was a prediction that Jesus' death would not be for Israel only, but for all the children of God scattered around the world.

So from that time on the Jewish leaders began plotting Jesus' death.

Jesus now stopped His public ministry. He went to the edge of the desert to the village of Ephraim and stayed there with His disciples.

From John 11:47-54

53
ONLY ONE
March, A.D. 30

Later as Jesus and His disciples continued onward toward Jerusalem, they reached the border between Galilee and Samaria and entered a village. Ten lepers stood at a distance crying out, "Jesus, Sir, have mercy on us!"

He glanced at them and said, "Go to the Jewish priest and show him that you are healed!" And as they were on their way, their leprosy disappeared!

One of them came back to Jesus, shouting, "Glory to God, I am healed!" He fell flat on the ground in front of Jesus, face downward in the dust, thanking Him for what He had done. (This man was a despised Samaritan.)

Jesus asked, "Didn't I heal ten men? Where are the nine? Does only this foreigner return to give glory to God?" And Jesus said to the man, "Stand up and go; your faith has made you well."

From Luke 17:11-19

Jesus told this story to some who boasted of all the good things they did and who thought they were better than everyone else: "Two men went to the Temple to pray. One was a proud, self-righteous Pharisee, and the other a cheating tax collector. The proud Pharisee prayed this prayer: 'Thank God, I am not a sinner like everyone else, especially like that tax collector over there! For I never cheat, I don't commit adultery, I go without food twice a week, and I give to God a tenth of everything I earn.' But the corrupt tax collector stood at a distance and dared not even lift his eyes to heaven as he prayed, but beat upon his chest in sorrow, exclaiming, 'God, be merciful to me, a sinner.'

"I tell you, this sinner—not the proud Pharisee—returned home forgiven! For the proud shall be humbled, but the humble shall be honored."

54

TO BOASTERS

From Luke 18:9-14

55
ENTRANCE REQUIREMENTS

One day some mothers brought their children to Jesus to touch and bless. But the disciples told them to go away. Then Jesus called the children over to Him and said to the disciples, "Let the little children come to Me! Never send them away! For the Kingdom of God belongs to men who have trusting hearts as these little children do. And anyone who doesn't have their kind of faith will never get within the Kingdom's gates!"

Once a Jewish religious leader asked Him this question: "Good Sir, what shall I do to get to heaven?"

"Do you realize what you are saying when you call me 'good'?" Jesus asked him. "Only God is truly good, and no one else. But as to your question, you know what the ten commandments say—don't commit adultery, don't murder, don't steal, don't lie, honor your parents, and so on."

The man replied, "I've obeyed every one of these laws since I was a small child."

Jesus felt genuine love for this man as He looked at him. Then He said, "There is still one thing you lack! Sell all you have and give the money to the poor—it will become treasure for you in heaven—and come, follow Me."

But when the man heard this, he went away sadly, for he was very rich.

Jesus watched him go and then said to His disciples, "It is so hard for the rich to enter the Kingdom of God! It is easier for a camel to go through the eye of a needle than for a rich man to enter the Kingdom of God."

Those who heard Him say this exclaimed, "If it is as hard as that, how can anyone be saved?"

He replied, "God can do what men can't!"

And Peter said, "We have left our homes and followed You."

"Yes," Jesus replied, "and everyone who has done as you have, leaving home, wife, brothers, parents, or children for the sake of the Kingdom of God, will be repaid many times over now, as well as receive eternal life in the world to come."

From Mark 10:21; Luke 18:15-30

56
BEGINNING THE DREADFUL JOURNEY

Jesus and His disciples were on the way to Jerusalem, and Jesus was walking along ahead; as the disciples were following, they were filled with terror and with dread. Gathering The Twelve around Him He told them, "As you know, we are going to Jerusalem. And when we get there, all the predictions of the ancient prophets concerning Me will come true. I, the Son of Man, will be arrested and taken before the chief priests and the Jewish leaders, who will sentence Me to die and hand Me over to the Romans to be killed. They will mock Me and spit on Me and flog Me with their whips and kill Me; and after three days I will come back to life again."

Then James and John, the sons of Zebedee, came over and spoke to Him in a low voice. "Master," they said, "we want You to do us a favor."

"What is it?" He asked.

"We want to sit on the thrones next to Yours in Your kingdom," they said, "one at Your right and the other at Your left!"

But Jesus answered, "You don't know what you are asking! Are you able to drink from the bitter cup of sorrow I must drink from? Or to be baptized with the baptism of suffering I must be baptized with?" "Oh, yes," they said, "we are!" And Jesus said, "You shall indeed drink from My cup and be baptized with My baptism, but I do not have the right to place you next to Me on My throne. Those appointments have already been made."

When the other disciples discovered what James and John had asked, they were very indignant. So Jesus called them to Him and said, "As you know, the kings and great men of the earth lord it over the people; but among you it is different. Whoever wants to be great among you must be your servant! And whoever wants to be greatest of all must be the slave of all. For even I, the Son of Man, am not here to be served, but to help others, and to give My life as a ransom for many."

From Mark 10:32-45; Luke 18:31

As Jesus was passing through Jericho, a man named Zacchaeus, one of the most influential Jews in the Roman tax-collecting business and of course a very rich man, tried to get a look at Jesus, but he was too short to see over the crowds. So he ran ahead and climbed into a sycamore tree beside the road to see Him and watched from there.

When Jesus came by He looked up at Zacchaeus and called him by name! "Zacchaeus," He said, "Quick! Come down! For I am going to be guest in your home today!" Zacchaeus climbed down hurriedly and took Jesus to his house in great excitement and joy.

But the crowds were displeased. "He has gone to be the guest of a notorious sinner," they grumbled.

Meanwhile Zacchaeus stood before the Lord and said, "Sir, from now on I will give half my wealth to the poor, and if I find I have overcharged anyone on his taxes, I will penalize myself by giving him back four times as much!"

Jesus told him, "This shows that salvation has come to this home today. This man was one of the lost sons of Abraham, and I, the Son of Man, have come to search for and save such souls as his."

From Luke 19:1-10

57
CHANGE OF HEART

58 FAITH ENOUGH

Late in March, A.D. 30

As Jesus and His disciples left the city of Jericho, a great crowd was following. Now it happened that a blind beggar named Bartimaeus (the son of Timaeus) was sitting beside the road as Jesus was going by. When

Bartimaeus heard that Jesus from Nazareth was near, he began to shout, "Jesus, Son of David, have mercy on me!"

"Shut up!" some of the people yelled at him.

But he only shouted the louder, again and again, "O, Son of David, have mercy on me!"

Jesus stopped in the road when He heard him and said, "Tell him to come here."

So they called the blind man. "You lucky fellow," they said, "come on, He is calling you!"

Bartimaeus yanked off his old coat and flung it aside, jumped up and came to Jesus.

"What do you want Me to do for you?" Jesus asked.

"O Teacher," the blind man said, "I want to see!"

And Jesus said to him, "All right, it's done! Your faith has healed you!" And instantly the blind man could see, and he followed Jesus down the road!

From Mark 10:46-52

WANTED!

The Passover, a Jewish holy day, was near, and many country people arrived in Jerusalem several days early so that they could go through the cleansing ceremony before the Passover began. They wanted to see Jesus, and as they gossiped in the Temple, they asked each other, "What do you think? Will He come for the Passover?"

Meanwhile the chief priests and Pharisees had publicly announced that anyone seeing Jesus must report Him immediately so that they could arrest Him.

From John 11:55-57

60
DINNER PARTY AT BETHANY
Saturday, April 1, A.D. 30

Six days before the Passover ceremonies began, Jesus arrived in Bethany where Lazarus was—the man He had brought back to life. A banquet was prepared in Jesus' honor at the home of Simon the leper. Martha served, and Lazarus sat at the table with Jesus.

Then Mary took a jar of costly perfume made from essence of nard and anointed Jesus' feet with it and wiped them with her hair. The house was filled with fragrance. But Judas Iscariot, one of His disciples—the one who would betray Him—said, "That perfume was worth a fortune! It should have been sold for $6,000 and the money given to the poor!" (Not that he cared for the poor, but he was in charge of the disciples' funds and often dipped into them for his own use!)

Jesus replied, "Let her alone. You can always help the poor, but I won't be with you very long! She has

done what she could, and has anointed My body ahead of time for burial. And I tell you this in solemn truth, that wherever the Good News is preached throughout the world, this woman's deed will be remembered and praised."

From Mark 14:3, 5, 8, 9; John 12:1-8

61
ALL ACCORDING TO PLAN
Sunday, April 2, A.D. 30

The next day, the news that Jesus was on the way to Jerusalem swept through the city.

When the ordinary people of Jerusalem heard of Jesus' arrival, they flocked to see Him, and also to see Lazarus—the man who had come back to life again. Then the chief priests decided to kill Lazarus too, for it was because of him that many of the Jewish leaders had deserted and believed in Jesus as their Messiah.

As Jesus and the disciples approached Jerusalem, near the village of Bethphage on the Mount of Olives, Jesus sent two of them into the village ahead. "Just as you enter," He said, "you will see a donkey tied, with its colt beside it. Untie them and bring them here. And if anyone asks you what you are doing, just say, 'The Master needs them,' and they will let them go." This was done to fulfill the ancient prophecy, "Tell Jerusalem her King is coming to her, riding humbly on a donkey's colt!"

The two disciples found the colt as Jesus said. And sure enough, as they were untying it, the owners demanded an explanation. "What are you doing?" they asked. "Why are you untying our colt?"

And the disciples simply replied, "The Lord needs him!" So they brought the colt to Jesus and threw some of their clothing across its back for Jesus to sit on.

Some of the crowd then threw down their garments along the road ahead of Him, and others cut branches from the trees and spread them out before Him. As they reached the place where the road started down from the

Mount of Olives, the whole procession began to shout and sing as they walked along, praising God for the wonderful miracles Jesus had done. "God has given us a King!" they exulted. "Long live the King! Let all heaven rejoice! Glory to God in the highest heavens!"

But some of the Pharisees among the crowd said, "Sir, rebuke your followers for saying things like that!"

He replied, "If they kept quiet, the stones along the road would burst into cheers!"

The entire city of Jerusalem was stirred as He entered. "Who is it?" they asked.

And the crowds replied, "This is the prophet Jesus from Nazareth in Galilee."

And so He entered Jerusalem, and went into the Temple. He looked carefully at everything around Him and then left—for now it was late in the afternoon—and went back to Bethany with the twelve disciples.

From Matthew 21:1-6, 8, 10, 11; Mark 11:11; Luke 19:32-40; John 12:9-12

62

MARKETPLACE, OR TEMPLE?
Monday, April 3, A.D. 30

When Jesus and His disciples arrived back in Jerusalem the next day, He went to the Temple and began to drive out the merchants and their customers. He knocked over the tables of the money changers and the stalls of those selling doves, and stopped everyone from bringing in loads of merchandise. He told them, "It is written in the Scriptures, 'My Temple is to be a place of prayer for all nations,' but you have turned it into a den of robbers."

And now the blind and crippled came to Him in the Temple, and He healed them there. But when the chief priests and other Jewish leaders saw these wonderful miracles and heard even the little children in the Temple shouting, "God bless the Son of David," they were disturbed and indignant and said to Him, "Do you hear what these children are saying?"

"Yes," Jesus told them. "Didn't you ever read the Scriptures? For they say, 'Even little babies shall praise Him!'"

When the chief priests and other Jewish leaders heard what He had done, they began planning how best to get rid of Him. Their problem was that they were afraid of riots, because the people were so enthusiastic about Jesus' teaching.

That evening, as usual, Jesus and His disciples left the city.

From Matthew 21:14-16; Mark 11:15-19

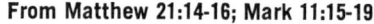

The next morning Jesus said to the disciples, "If you only have faith in God—this is the absolute truth—you can say to this Mount of Olives, 'Rise up and fall into the Mediterranean,' and your command will be obeyed. All that's required is that you really believe and have no doubt! Listen to Me! You can pray for anything, and if you believe you have it, it's yours! But when you are praying, forgive anyone you are holding a grudge against, so that your Father in heaven may forgive you your sins."

When He had returned to the Temple and was teaching, the chief priests and other Jewish leaders came up to Him and demanded to know by whose authority He had thrown the merchants out of the Temple the day before.

"I'll tell you if you answer one question first," Jesus replied. "Was John the Baptist sent from God, or not?"

They talked it over among themselves. "If we say, 'From God,' then He will ask why we didn't believe John. And if we deny that God sent him, we'll be mobbed, for this crowd all think he was a prophet." So they finally replied, "We don't know!"

And Jesus said, "Then I won't answer your question either!"

From Matthew 21:23-27; Mark 11:20, 22-25

63
UNANSWERED QUESTION
Tuesday, April 4, A.D. 30

64
TRICK QUESTIONS

Then the Pharisees called a meeting to think of some way to trap Jesus into saying something for which they could arrest Him. They decided to send some of their men along with the Herodians to ask Him this question: "Sir, we know You are very honest and teach the truth regardless of the consequences, without fear or favor. Now tell us, is it right to pay taxes to the Roman government or not?"

But Jesus saw what they were after. "You hypocrites!" He said. "Whom are you trying to fool with your trick questions? Here, show Me a coin." And they handed Him a penny.

"Whose picture is on it?" He asked them. "And whose name is this beneath the picture?"

"Caesar's," they replied.

"Well then," He said, "give it to Caesar if it is his and give God everything that belongs to God." His reply surprised and baffled them and they went away.

The crowds were profoundly impressed by His answers—but not the Pharisees! When they heard He had routed the Sadducees with His reply, they thought up a fresh question of their own to ask Him. One of them, a lawyer, spoke up, "Sir, which is the most important command in the laws of Moses?"

Jesus replied, " 'Love the Lord your God with all your heart, soul and mind.' This is the great first commandment. The second in importance is similar, 'Love your neighbor as much as you love yourself.' All the other commandments and all the demands of the prophets stem from these two laws, and are fulfilled in them. Keep them and you are obeying all the others."

From Matthew 22:15-22, 33-40

But despite all the miracles Jesus had done, most of the people would not believe He was the Messiah. (This is exactly what Isaiah the prophet had predicted: "Lord, who will believe us? Who will accept God's mighty miracles as proof?")

However, many of the Jewish leaders believed Jesus to be the Messiah but wouldn't admit it to anyone because of their fear that the Pharisees would excommunicate them from the synagogue, for they loved the praise of men more than the praise of God.

Every day during this Passover season Jesus went to the Temple to teach, and the crowds began gathering early in the morning to hear Him. And each evening He returned to spend the night on the Mount of Olives.

"Don't let anyone mislead you," Jesus told the people. "For many will come announcing themselves as the Messiah, and saying, 'The time has come.' Don't you believe them!

"Then if anyone tells you, 'The Messiah has arrived at such and such a place, or has appeared here or there or in the village yonder,' don't believe it. For false Christs shall arise, and false prophets, and will do wonderful miracles, so that if it were possible, even God's chosen ones would be deceived. See, I have warned you.

"So if someone tells you the Messiah has returned and is out in the desert, don't bother to go and look. Or, that He is hiding at a certain place, don't believe it! For as the lightning flashes across the sky from east to west, so shall My coming be, when I—the Son of Man—return."

AS LIGHTNING FLASHES

From Matthew 24:23-27; Luke 21:8, 37, 38; John 12:37, 38, 42, 43

66
SIGNALS

Then Jesus said to the crowds, and to His disciples, "At the last there will appear a signal in the heavens of My coming; and there will be deep mourning all around the earth. And the nations of the world will see Me arrive in the clouds of heaven, with power and great glory. And I shall send forth My angels with the sound of a mighty trumpet blast, and they will gather My chosen ones from the farthest ends of the earth and heaven.

"And when you hear of wars and insurrections beginning, don't panic. True, wars must come, but the end won't follow immediately—for nation shall rise against nation and kingdom against kingdom, and there will be great earthquakes, and famines in many lands, and epidemics, and terrifying things happening in the heavens.

"Then there will be strange events in the skies—warnings, evil omens and portents in the sun, moon and stars; and down here on earth the nations will be in turmoil, perplexed by the roaring seas and strange tides. The courage of many people will falter because of the fearful fate they see coming upon the earth, for the stability of the very heavens will be broken up.

"So when all these things begin to happen, stand straight and look up! For your salvation is near.

"And the Good News about the Kingdom will be preached in the whole world, so that all nations will hear it, and then, finally, the end will come."

From Matthew 24:14, 30, 31; Luke 21:9-11, 25, 26, 28

When Jesus had finished saying all these things, He told His disciples, "As you know, the Passover celebration begins in two days, and I shall be betrayed and crucified."

At that very moment, the chief priests and other Jewish officials were meeting at the residence of Caiaphas, the high priest, to discuss ways of capturing Jesus quietly, and killing Him. "But not during the Passover celebration," they agreed, "for there would be a riot."

Then one of the twelve apostles—Judas Iscariot—went to the chief priests, and asked, "How much will

67
BLOOD MONEY

you pay me to get Jesus into your hands?" And they gave him thirty silver coins. From that time on, Judas watched for an opportunity to betray Jesus to them when the crowds weren't around.

From Matthew 26:1-5, 14-16; Luke 22:6

68

SUPPER FOR THIRTEEN MEN

Thursday evening, April 6, A.D. 30

Now the day of the Passover celebration arrived when the Passover lamb was killed and eaten with the unleavened bread. Jesus sent Peter and John ahead to find a place to prepare their Passover meal.

"Where do You want us to go?" they asked.

And He replied, "As soon as you enter Jerusalem, you will see a man walking along carrying a pitcher of water. Follow him into the house he enters and say to the man who lives there, 'Our Teacher says for you to show us the guest room where He can eat the Passover meal with His disciples.' He will take you upstairs to a large room all ready for us. That is the place. Go ahead and prepare the meal there."

They went off to the city and found everything just as Jesus had said. And they prepared the Passover supper. Jesus and the others arrived, and at the proper time all sat down together at the table, and He said, "I have looked forward to this hour with deep longing, anxious to eat this Passover meal with you before My suffering begins. For I tell you now that I won't eat it again until all it represents has taken place in the Kingdom of God."

Then He took a glass of wine; and when He had given thanks for it He said, "Take this and share it among yourselves. For I will not drink wine again until the Kingdom of God has come."

As they were eating, Jesus took a small loaf of bread and blessed it and broke it apart and gave it to the disciples and said, "Take it and eat it, for this is My body!"

From Matthew 26:26; Luke 22:7-18

69
A NIGHT TO REMEMBER

Jesus knew on the evening of Passover Day that it would be His last night on earth before returning to His Father. And how He loved His disciples! So He got up from the supper table, took off His robe and wrapped a towel around His loins. Then, He poured water into a basin and began to wash the disciples' feet and to wipe them with the towel He had around Him.

When He came to Simon Peter, Peter said to Him, "Master, You shouldn't be washing our feet like this!"

Jesus replied, "You don't understand now why I am doing it; some day you will."

"No," Peter protested, "You shall never wash my feet!"

"But if I don't, you can't be My partner," Jesus replied.

Simon Peter exclaimed, "Then wash my hands and head as well—not just my feet!"

Jesus replied, "One who has bathed all over needs only his feet washed to be entirely clean! Now you are clean—but that isn't true of everyone here." For Jesus knew who would betray Him. That is what He meant when He said, "Not all of you are clean."

After washing their feet, He put on His robe again and sat down and asked, "Do you understand what I was doing? You call Me 'Master' and 'Lord,' and you do

well to say it, for it is true. And since I, the Lord and Teacher, have washed your feet, you ought to wash each other's feet. I have given you an example to follow: do as I have done to you.

"I am not saying these things to all of you; I know so well each one of you I chose. The Scripture declares, 'One who eats supper with Me will betray Me,' and this will soon come true. I tell you this now so that when it happens, you will believe on Me."

A great sadness swept over them, and one by one they asked Him, "Am I the one?"

He replied, "It is one of you twelve eating with Me now. I must die, as the prophets declared long ago; but, oh, the misery ahead for the man by whom I am betrayed. Oh, that he had never been born!"

The other disciples looked at each other, wondering whom He could mean. John happened to be next to Jesus at the table since he was His close friend. Simon Peter motioned to him to ask Jesus who it was who would do this terrible deed. So he leaned around and asked Him, "Lord, who is it?"

Jesus told him, "It is the one I honor by giving the bread dipped in the sauce." And when He had dipped it, He gave it to Judas, son of Simon Iscariot. And when Judas had eaten it, Satan entered into him. Then Jesus told him, "Hurry—do it now." None of the others at the table knew what Jesus meant. Some thought that since Judas was their treasurer, Jesus was telling him to go and pay for the food or to give some money to the poor. Judas left at once, going out into the night.

From Mark 14:19-21; John 13:1, 3-15, 18, 19, 22-30

70

FINAL INSTRUCTIONS

As soon as Judas left the room, Jesus said, "My time has come; the glory of God will soon surround Me—and God shall receive great praise because of all that happens to Me. And God shall give Me His own glory, and this so very soon.

"Dear, dear children, how brief are these moments before I must go away and leave you! Then, though you search for Me, you cannot come to Me—just as I told the Jewish leaders. And so I am giving a new commandment to you now—love each other just as much as I love you. Your strong love for each other will prove to the world that you are My disciples."

Simon Peter said, "Master, where are You going?"

And Jesus replied, "You can't go with Me now; but you will follow Me later."

Then Jesus said to all of them, "Tonight you will all desert me. For it is written in the Scriptures that God will smite the Shepherd, and the sheep of the flock shall be scattered. But after I have been brought to life again, I will go to Galilee, and meet you there."

But Peter said, "If everyone else deserts You, I won't!"

Jesus told him, "The truth is that this very night, before the cock crows at dawn, you will deny Me three times!"

But Peter insisted, "I would die first!" And all the other disciples said the same thing.

From Matthew 26:31-35; John 13:31-36

71
HEAVENLY PLANS

"Don't be upset. Trust God—and trust Me. There are many homes up there where My Father lives, and I am going to get them ready for your coming! When they are all ready, I will come back and get you and take you with Me; then you will be where I am. I would tell you plainly if this were not so. And you know how to get where I am going."

"No, we don't," Thomas said. "We don't even know where You are going—how can we know the way?"

Jesus told him, "I am the Way—yes, and the Truth and the Life. No one can get to the Father except by means of Me. If you had known who I am, then you would have known who My Father is! From now on you know Him—and have seen Him!"

Philip said, "Lord, show us the Father and we will be satisfied."

Jesus replied, "Don't you even yet know who I am, Philip, even after all this time I have been with you? Anyone who has seen Me has seen the Father! So why are you asking to see Him? Don't you believe that I am in the Father and the Father is in Me?

"The words I say are not My own, but are from My Father who lives in Me! And He does His work through Me. Just believe it—that I am in the Father and the Father is in Me. Or else believe it because of the mighty miracles you have seen Me do.

"In solemn truth I tell you, anyone believing in Me shall do the same miracles I have done, and even greater ones, because I am going to be with the Father. You can ask Him for anything, using My name, and I will do it, for this will bring praise to the Father because of what I, the Son, will do for you. Yes, ask anything, using My name, and I will do it!"

From John 14:1-14

"In just a little while I will be gone from the world, but I will still be present with you. For I will live again—and you will too.

"The one who obeys Me is the one who loves Me; and because he loves Me, My Father will love him; and I will love him too, and I will reveal Myself to him. I will only reveal Myself to those who love Me and obey Me.

"When the Father sends the Comforter to represent Me—and by the Comforter I mean the Holy Spirit—He will teach you much more as well as remind you of everything I Myself have told you.

"I am leaving you with a gift—peace of mind and heart! And the peace I give isn't fragile like the peace the world gives! So don't be troubled or afraid. Remember what I told you—I am going away, but I will come back again to you. I have told you these things before they happen so that when they do, you will believe in Me.

"I don't have much more time to talk to you, for the evil prince of this world is on the way. He has no power

72

TIME RUNNING OUT

over Me, but I will freely do what the Father requires of Me so that the world will know that I love the Father."

When Jesus had finished saying all these things, He looked up to heaven and said, "Father, the time has come. Reveal the glory of Your Son so that He can give the glory back to You. For You have given Him authority over every man and woman in all the earth. He gives eternal life to each one You have given Him. And this is the only way to have eternal life—by knowing You, the only true God, and Jesus Christ, the one You sent to earth!"

Then, accompanied by the disciples, Jesus left the upstairs room and went to the Mount of Olives.

From Luke 22:39; John 14:19, 21, 23, 26-31; 17:1-3

73
AGONY IN A GARDEN

Then Jesus brought the disciples to a garden grove called Gethsemane, and told them to sit down and wait while He went on ahead to pray. He took Peter with Him and Zebedee's two sons James and John. He began to be filled with anguish and despair. He said to them, "My soul is crushed by sorrow to the point of death. Stay here and watch with Me."

He went forward a little farther and fell to the ground, and prayed that if it were possible the awful hour awaiting Him might never come. "Father! Father!" He said, "everything is possible for You. Take away this cup from Me. Yet I want Your will, not Mine."

Then an angel from heaven appeared and strengthened Him. For He was in such agony of spirit that He broke into a sweat of blood, with great drops falling to the ground as He prayed more and more earnestly.

Then He returned to the three disciples and found them asleep. "Simon!" He said. "Asleep? Couldn't you watch with Me for even an hour? Watch with Me and pray, lest the Tempter overpower you. For though the spirit is willing enough, the body is weak."

Again He left them and prayed, "My Father! If this cup cannot go away until I drink it all, Your will be done." He returned to them again and found them sleeping, for their eyes were heavy, so He went back to prayer the third time, saying the same things again.

Then He came back to the disciples and said to them, "Sleep on now and take your rest. But no! The time has come! I am betrayed into the hands of evil men!"

But even as He said this, a mob approached, led by Judas, one of His twelve disciples.

From Matthew 26:36, 37, 42-45; Mark 14:34-38; Luke 22:43, 44, 47

74
ARRESTED AND DESERTED

Judas, the betrayer, knew the place called Gethsemane, for Jesus had gone there many times with His disciples. The chief priests and Pharisees had given Judas a squad of soldiers and police to accompany him. Now, with blazing torches, lanterns and weapons, they arrived at the olive grove. Jesus fully realized all that was going to happen to Him. Stepping forward to meet them He asked, "Who are you looking for?"

"Jesus of Nazareth," they replied.

"I am He," Jesus said. And as He said it, they all fell backwards to the ground!

Once more He asked them, "For whom are you searching?"

And again they replied, "Jesus of Nazareth."

"I told you I am He," Jesus said; "and since I am the one you are after, let these others go."

Judas had told the soldiers and police, "You will know which one to arrest when I go over and embrace Him. Then you can take Him easily." So now Judas came straight to Jesus. "Master," he exclaimed, and embraced Him with a great show of friendliness and kissed Him on the cheek.

But Jesus said, "Judas, how can you do this—betray the Messiah with a kiss?" Then the mob arrested Jesus and held Him fast.

When the other disciples saw what was about to happen, they exclaimed, "Master, shall we fight? We brought along the swords!" Then Simon Peter drew a sword and slashed off the right ear of Malchus, the High Priest's servant.

But Jesus said to Peter, "Don't resist anymore. Put away your sword. Those using swords will get killed. Don't you realize that I could ask My Father for thousands of angels to protect us, and He would send them instantly? But if I did, how would the Scriptures be fulfilled that describe the events now happening?" Then Jesus touched the place where the man's ear had been and restored it.

Jesus spoke to the crowd saying, "Am I some dangerous criminal, that you had to arm yourselves with swords and clubs before you could arrest Me? I was with you teaching daily in the Temple and you didn't stop Me then. But this is all happening to fulfill the words of the prophets as recorded in the Scriptures." At that point, all the disciples deserted Him and fled.

From Matthew 26:49, 52-56; Mark 14:44-46; Luke 22:47-49, 51; John 18:2-8, 10, 11

75
GUILTY!
Friday, 3:00 - 6:00 A.M.

First the soldiers took Jesus to Annas, the father-in-law of Caiaphas, the High Priest that year. (Caiaphas was the one who told the other Jewish leaders, "Better that one should die for all.") Then Annas sent Jesus, bound, to Caiaphas the High Priest.

Meanwhile Peter was following far to the rear, and came to the courtyard of the High Priest's house as did another of the disciples who was acquainted with the High Priest. So that disciple was permitted into the courtyard along with Jesus, while Peter stood outside the gate. Then the other disciple spoke to the girl watching at the gate, and she let Peter in.

The girl asked Peter, "Aren't you one of Jesus' disciples?"

"No," he said, "I am not!"

The police and the household servants were standing around a fire they had made, for it was cold. And Peter stood there with them, warming himself.

Inside, the High Priest began asking Jesus about His followers and what He had been teaching them. Jesus replied, "What I teach is widely known, for I have preached regularly in the synagogue and Temple; I have been heard by all the Jewish leaders and teach nothing in private that I have not said in public. Why are you asking Me this question? Ask those who heard Me. You have some of them here. They know what I said."

One of the soldiers standing there struck Jesus with his fist. "Is that the way to answer the High Priest?" he demanded.

"If I lied, prove it," Jesus said. "Should you hit a man for telling the truth?"

The chief priests and, in fact, the entire Jewish Supreme Court assembled there and looked for witnesses who would lie about Jesus, in order to build a case against Him that would result in a death sentence. But even though they found many false witnesses, these always contradicted each other, until they found two men who declared, "This man said, 'I am able to destroy the Temple of God and rebuild it in three days!'"

Then the High Priest stood up and said to Jesus, "Well, what about it? Did You say that, or didn't You?" But Jesus remained silent. Then the High Priest said to Him, "I demand in the name of the living God that You tell us whether You claim to be the Messiah, the Son of God."

"Yes," Jesus said, "I am. And in the future you will see Me, the Son of Man, sitting at the right hand of God and returning on the clouds of heaven."

Then the High Priest tore at his own clothing, shouting, "Blasphemy! What need have we for other witnesses? You have all heard Him say it! What is your verdict?"

They answered, "Give Him death."

Then some of them began to spit at Him, and they blindfolded Him and began to hammer His face with their fists. "Who hit You that time, You prophet?" they jeered. And even the bailiffs were slapping His face as they led Him away.

From Matthew 26:58-66; Mark 14:65; John 18:13-23

76

SOUND OF THE ROOSTER

Meanwhile Peter was below in the courtyard. One of the maids who worked for the High Priest noticed Peter warming himself at the fire. She looked at him closely and then announced, "You were with Jesus, the Nazarene."

Peter denied it. "I don't know what you're talking about!" he said, and walked over to the edge of the courtyard. Just then, a rooster crowed.

Later one of the household slaves of the High Priest—a relative of the man whose ear Peter had cut off—asked, "Didn't I see you out there in the olive grove with Jesus?" Again Peter denied it.

Others standing around the fire began saying to Peter, "You are one of them, too, for you are from Galilee!"

Peter began to curse and swear. "I don't even know this fellow you are talking about," he said. And immediately the rooster crowed the second time.

At that moment Jesus turned and looked at Peter. Suddenly Jesus' words flashed through Peter's mind, "Before the rooster crows at dawn twice, you will deny Me three times." And Peter walked out of the courtyard and started crying bitterly.

From Matthew 26:34; Mark 14:66-68, 70-72; Luke 22:61, 62; John 18:26, 27

77
FIELD OF BLOOD

About that time Judas, who betrayed Jesus, when he saw that He had been condemned to die, changed his mind and deeply regretted what he had done, and brought back the money to the chief priests and other Jewish leaders.

"I have sinned," he declared, "for I betrayed an innocent man."

"That's your problem," they retorted. Then he threw the money onto the floor of the Temple and went out and hanged himself.

The chief priests picked the money up. "We can't put it in the collection," they said, "since it's against our laws to accept money paid for murder." They talked it over and finally decided to buy a certain field, where the clay was used by potters, and to make it into a cemetery for foreigners who died in Jerusalem. That is why the cemetery is still called "The Field of Blood."

This fulfilled the prophecy of Jeremiah which says, "They took the thirty pieces of silver—the price at which He was valued by the people of Israel—and purchased a field from the potters; as the Lord directed me."

From Matthew 27:3-10

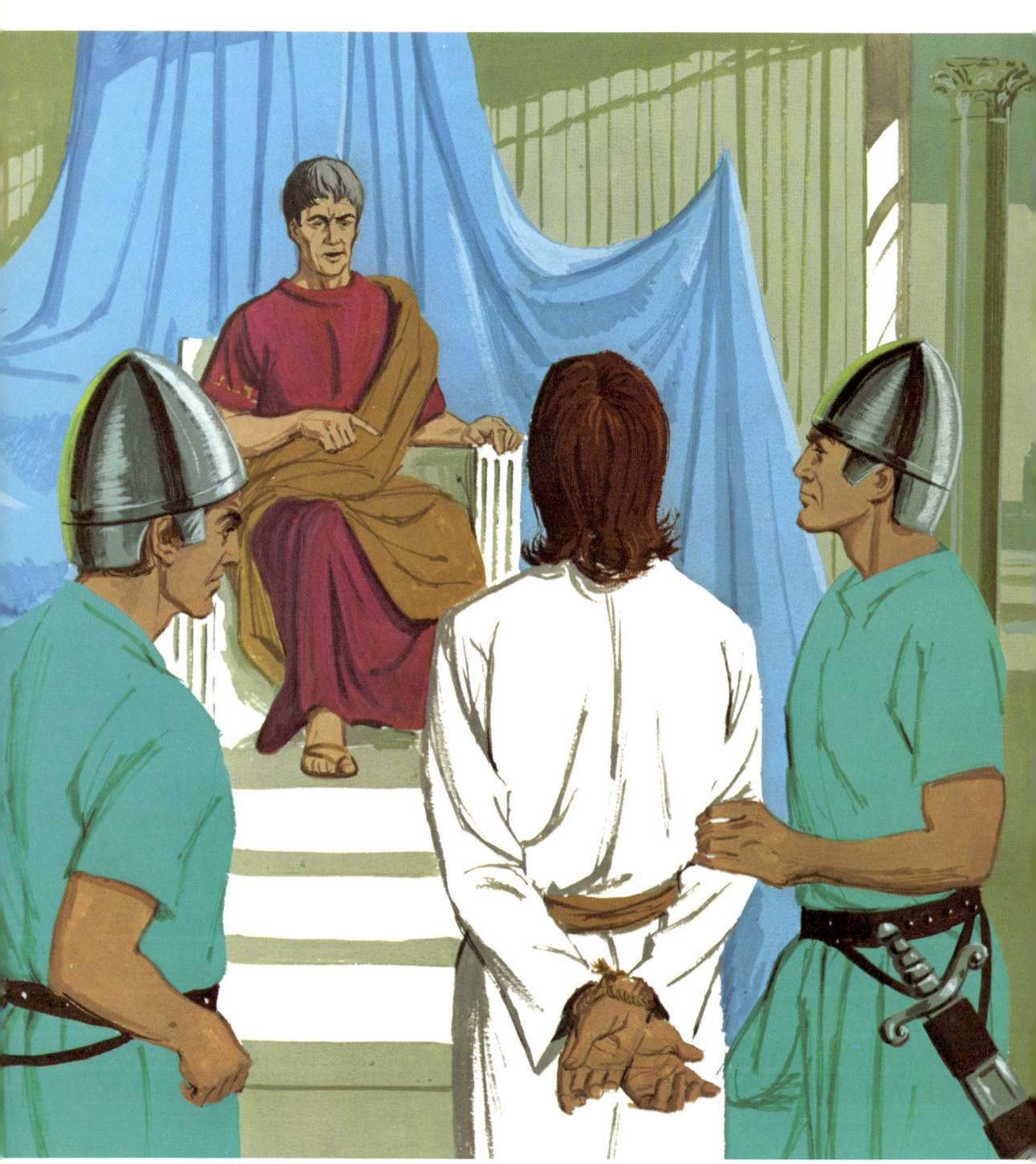

78
NOTHING MORE TO SAY
Friday morning, 6:00 - 9:00 A.M.

Jesus' trial before Caiaphas ended in the early hours of the morning. Then the entire Council took Jesus over to the palace of Pilate, the governor.

Jesus' accusers wouldn't go in themselves for that would "defile" them, they said, and they wouldn't be allowed to eat the Passover lamb. So Pilate, the governor, went out to them and asked, "What is your charge against this man? What are you accusing Him of doing?"

They replied, "We wouldn't have brought Him to you if He weren't a criminal!"

"Then take Him away and judge Him yourselves by your own laws," Pilate told them.

"But we want Him crucified," they said, "and your approval is required." This fulfilled Jesus' prediction concerning the method of His execution.

Then Pilate went back into the palace and called for Jesus to be brought to him. "Are you the King of the Jews?" he asked Him.

" 'King,' as you use the word or as the Jews use it?" Jesus asked.

"Am I a Jew?" Pilate retorted. "Your own people and their chief priests brought You here. Why? What have You done?"

Then Jesus answered, "I am not an earthly king. If I were, My followers would have fought when I was arrested by the Jewish leaders. But My Kingdom is not of the world."

Pilate replied, "But You are a King then?"

"Yes," Jesus said. "I was born for that purpose. And I came to bring truth to the world. All who love the truth are My followers."

"What is truth?" Pilate exclaimed. Then he went out again to the people and told them, "He is not guilty of any crime."

Then the chief priests accused Him of many crimes, and Pilate asked Him, "Why don't You say something? What about all these charges against You?" But Jesus said nothing more, much to Pilate's amazement.

They became desperate! "But He is causing riots against the government everywhere He goes—all over Judea, from Galilee to Jerusalem!"

"Is He then a Galilean?" Pilate asked. When they told him yes, Pilate said to take Him to King Herod, for Galilee was under Herod's jurisdiction; and Herod happened to be in Jerusalem at the time.

Herod was delighted at the opportunity to see Jesus, for he had heard a lot about Him and had been hoping to see Him perform a miracle. He asked Jesus question after question, but there was no reply. Meanwhile the chief priests and the other religious leaders stood there shouting their accusations.

Now Herod and his soldiers began mocking and ridiculing Jesus; and putting a kingly robe on Him, they sent Him back to Pilate. That day Herod and Pilate—enemies before—became fast friends.

Then Pilate called together the chief priests and other Jewish leaders, along with the people, and announced his verdict: "You brought this man to me, accusing Him of leading a revolt against the Roman government. I have examined Him thoroughly on this point and find Him innocent. Herod came to the same conclusion and sent Him back to us. Nothing this man has done calls for the death penalty."

From Mark 15:3-5; Luke 23:1, 5-15; John 18:28-38

Now the Roman governor's custom was to release one Jewish prisoner each year during the Passover celebration, anyone the people wanted. This year there was a particularly notorious criminal in jail named Barabbas. He was in prison with others for murdering a man during an insurrection. And as the crowds gathered before Pilate's house that morning he asked them, "Which shall I release to you—Barabbas, or Jesus, your Messiah?" For he knew very well that the Jewish leaders had arrested Jesus out of envy because of His popularity with the people.

Just then, as Pilate was presiding over the court, his wife sent him this message: "Leave that good man alone; for I had a terrible nightmare concerning Him last night."

Meanwhile the chief priests and Jewish officials persuaded the crowds to ask for Barabbas' release, and for Jesus' death. So when the governor said again, "Which of these two shall I release to you?"

The crowd replied, "Barabbas!"

"Then what shall I do with Jesus, your Messiah?" Pilate asked.

And they shouted, "Crucify Him!"

"Why?" Pilate demanded. "What has He done wrong?"

But they kept shouting, "Crucify! Crucify!"

Now a mighty roar rose from the crowd as with one voice they shouted, "Kill Him, and release Barabbas to

79
EXCHANGED FOR A MURDERER

us!" Pilate argued with them, for he wanted to release Jesus. But they shouted, "Crucify Him! Crucify Him!"

Once more, for the third time, he demanded, "Why? What crime has He committed? I have found no reason to sentence Him to death. I will therefore scourge Him and let Him go."

Then Pilate laid open Jesus' back with a leaded whip, and the soldiers made a crown of thorns and placed it on His head and robed Him in royal purple. Then they bowed low before Him. "Hail, 'King of the Jews!'" they mocked, and struck Him with their fists.

Pilate went outside again and said to the Jews, "I am going to bring Him out to you now, but understand clearly that I find Him not guilty."

Then Jesus came out wearing the crown of thorns and the purple robe. And Pilate said, "Behold the man!" At sight of Him the chief priests and Jewish officials began yelling, "Crucify! Crucify!"

"You crucify Him," Pilate said. "I find Him not guilty."

They replied, "By our laws He ought to die because He called Himself the Son of God."

When Pilate heard this, he was more frightened than ever. He took Jesus back into the palace again and asked Him, "Where are You from?" But Jesus gave no answer.

"You won't talk to me?" asked Pilate. "Don't You realize that I have the power to release You or to crucify You?"

Then Jesus said, "You would have no power at all over Me unless it were given to you from above! So those who brought Me to you have the greater sin."

Then Pilate tried to release Him, but the Jewish leaders told him, "If you release this man, you are no friend of Caesar's. Anyone who declares himself a king is a rebel against Caesar." At these words Pilate brought Jesus out to them again and sat down at the judgment bench on the stone-paved platform.

It was now about noon of the day before Passover. And Pilate said to the Jews, "Here is your King!"

"Away with Him," they yelled. "Away with Him—crucify Him!"

"What? Crucify your King?" Pilate asked.

"We have no king but Caesar," the chief priests shouted back.

When Pilate saw that he wasn't getting anywhere, and that a riot was developing, he sent for a bowl of water and washed his hands before the crowd, saying, "I am innocent of the blood of this good man. The responsibility is yours!"

And the mob yelled back, "His blood be on us and on our children!"

Then Pilate released Barabbas to them and gave them Jesus to be crucified.

From Matthew 27:15-26; Mark 15:7; Luke 23:17, 18, 20-22; John 19:1-16

80
PLACE OF THE SKULL
Friday morning, April 7, A.D. 30

The Roman soldiers took off the purple robe and put Jesus' own garment on Him again, and took Him out to be crucified.

As the crowd led Jesus away to His death, Simon of Cyrene, who was just coming into Jerusalem from the country, was forced to follow, carrying Jesus' cross.

Great crowds trailed along behind, and many grief-stricken women. And they brought Jesus to a place called Golgotha (the name means Place of a Skull) where the soldiers gave Him drugged wine to drink. But when He had tasted it, He refused.

"Father, forgive these people," Jesus said, "for they don't know what they are doing."

And Pilate posted a sign above Him reading, "JESUS OF NAZARETH, THE KING OF THE JEWS." The place where Jesus was crucified was near the city; and the signboard was written in Hebrew, Latin and Greek, so that many people read it.

Then the chief priests said to Pilate, "Change it from 'The King of the Jews' to '*He said*, I am King of the Jews.'"

Pilate replied, "What I have written, I have written. It stays exactly as it is."

And when they had crucified Him, they threw dice to divide His clothes among them. But they said, "Let's not tear up His robe." For it was seamless. "We'll throw dice to see who gets it." This fulfilled the Scripture that says, "They divided My clothes among them, and cast lots for My robe" (Psalm 22:18). And that is what they did. Then they sat around and watched Him as He hung there.

From Matthew 27:31, 34-36; Mark 15:22; Luke 23:26, 27, 34; John 19:19-25

81 BETWEEN TWO ROBBERS

Two robbers were also crucified that morning. (It was about nine o'clock in the morning when the crucifixion took place.) Their crosses were on either side of Jesus. And so the Scripture was fulfilled that said, "He was counted among evil men."

And the people passing by hurled abuse, shaking their heads at Him and saying, "So! You can destroy the Temple and build it again in three days, can You? Well then, come on down from the cross if You are the Son of God!"

And the chief priests and Jewish leaders mocked Him too. "He saved others," they scoffed, "but He can't save Himself! So You are the King of Israel, are You? Come down from the cross and we'll believe You! He trusted God—let God show His approval by delivering Him! Didn't He say, 'I am God's Son'?"

One of the criminals hanging beside Him scoffed, "So You're the Messiah, are You? Prove it by saving Yourself—and us too, while You're at it!"

But the other criminal protested. "Don't you even fear God when you are dying? We deserve to die for our evil deeds, but this man hasn't done one thing wrong." Then he said, "Jesus, remember me when You come into Your Kingdom."

And Jesus replied, "Today you will be with Me in Paradise. This is a solemn promise."

Standing near the cross were Jesus' mother, Mary, His aunt, the wife of Cleopas, and Mary Magdalene. When Jesus saw His mother standing beside John, His close friend, He said to her, "He is your son." And to John He said, "She is your mother!" And from then on John took her into his home.

From Matthew 27:39-43; Mark 15:25, 27, 28; Luke 23:39-43; John 19:25-27

82
DARKNESS, DEATH AND DESTRUCTION

About noon, darkness fell across the entire land, lasting until three o'clock that afternoon. Then Jesus called out with a loud voice, "Eloi, Eloi, lama sabachthani?" ("My God, My God, why have You deserted Me?")

Some of the people listening thought He was calling for the prophet Elijah!

Jesus knew that everything was now finished, and to

fulfill the Scriptures said, "I'm thirsty." A jar of sour wine was sitting there, so a sponge was soaked in it and put on a hyssop branch and held up to His lips. When Jesus had tasted it, He said, "It is finished." Then Jesus shouted out again, "Father, I commit My spirit to You," and with those words He died.

And look! The curtain secluding the Holiest Place in

the Temple was split apart from top to bottom; and the earth shook, and rocks broke. And tombs opened and many godly men and women who had died came back to life again, and left the cemetery after Jesus' resurrection, and went into Jerusalem, and appeared to many.

The soldiers at the crucifixion and the captain of the Roman military unit handling the executions were terribly frightened by the earthquake and all that happened. They exclaimed, "Surely this man was innocent. This was God's son."

And many women who had come down from Galilee with Jesus to care for Him were watching from a distance. Among them were Mary Magdalene and Mary the mother of James and Joseph, and the mother of James and John (the sons of Zebedee).

From Matthew 27:51-56; Mark 15:33-35; Luke 23:46, 47; John 19:28-30

83
SPICES AND TENDER HANDS

The Jewish leaders didn't want the victims hanging there alive the next day, which was the Sabbath (a very special Sabbath at that, for it was the Passover). So they asked Pilate to order the legs of the men broken, to hasten death; then their bodies could be taken down. So the soldiers came and broke the legs of the two men crucified with Jesus; but when they came to Him, they saw that He was dead already, and they didn't break His legs. However, one of the soldiers pierced His side with a spear, and blood and water flowed out.

The soldiers did this in fulfilment of the Scripture that says, "Not one of His bones shall be broken," and "They shall look on Him they pierced."

Then a man named Joseph, a member of the Jewish Supreme Court, from the city of Arimathea in Judea, went to Pilate and asked for the body of Jesus. He was a godly man who had been expecting the Messiah's coming and had not agreed with the decision and actions of the other Jewish leaders. Pilate couldn't believe that Jesus was already dead, so he called for the Roman officer in charge and asked him. The officer confirmed the fact, and Pilate told Joseph he could have the body.

Nicodemus (the man who had come to Jesus at night) came bringing a hundred pounds of embalming ointment made from myrrh and aloes. Together Nicodemus and Joseph wrapped Jesus' body in a long linen cloth saturated with the spices, as is the Jewish custom of burial.

The place of crucifixion was near a grove of trees where there was a new tomb, never used before. And so, because of the need for haste before the Sabbath, and because the tomb was close at hand, the two men laid Him there and rolled a stone in front of the entrance.

Both Mary Magdalene and the other Mary were sitting nearby watching. Then they went home and prepared spices and ointments to embalm Him. But by the time they were finished it was the Sabbath, so they rested all that day, as required by the Jewish law.

From Matthew 27:61; Mark 15:44-46; Luke 23:50-52, 56; John 19:31-34, 36, 37, 39-42

84
BROKEN SEAL

Saturday (the Jewish Sabbath), April 8, A.D. 30

The next day—at the close of the first day of the Passover ceremonies—the chief priests and Pharisees went to Pilate and told him, "Sir, that liar once said, 'After three days I will come back to life again.' So we request an order from you, sealing the tomb until the third day, to prevent His disciples from coming and stealing His body and then telling everyone He came back to life! If that happens we'll be worse off than we were at first."

"Use your own Temple police," Pilate told them. "They can guard it safely enough!" So they did, sealing the stone and leaving guards to protect it from intrusion.

But there was a sudden great earthquake. An angel of the Lord came down from heaven and rolled aside the stone and sat on it! His face shone like lightning and his clothing was a brilliant white. The guards shook with fear when they saw him, and fell into a dead faint.

From Matthew 27:62-66; 28:2-4

When the Sabbath ended, Mary Magdalene and Salome and Mary, the mother of James, and several others took the spices and ointments they had purchased to the tomb. On their way they were discussing how they could ever roll aside the huge stone from the entrance. But when they arrived they looked up and saw that the stone—a very heavy one—was already moved away and the entrance was open, but the body of the Lord Jesus was gone! Mary Magdalene ran and found Simon Peter and John and said, "They have taken the Lord's body out of the tomb, and I don't know where they have put Him!"

The other women went into the tomb. They stood there puzzled, trying to think what could have happened to it.

Suddenly two men appeared before them, clothed in shining robes so bright their eyes were dazzled. The women were terrified and bowed deeply before them.

Then the men asked, "Why are you looking in a tomb for someone who is alive? He isn't here! He has come back to life again! Don't you remember what He told

85
FIRST TO KNOW
Sunday, April 9, A.D. 30

you back in Galilee—that the Messiah must be betrayed into the power of evil men and be crucified and that He would rise again the third day? Look, that's where His body was lying! Now go and give this message to His disciples including Peter! Jesus is going ahead of you to Galilee. You will see Him there, just as He told you before He died."

Then the women remembered and ran from the tomb, badly frightened, but also filled with joy. They rushed to find the disciples to give them the angel's message.

Peter and John ran to the tomb to see. John outran Peter and got there first. He stooped and looked in and saw the linen cloth lying there, but he didn't go in. Then Peter arrived and went on inside. He also saw the cloth lying there, with the swath that had covered Jesus' head, rolled up in a bundle and lying at the side. Then John went in, too, and saw, and believed that He had risen, for until then they hadn't realized that the Scriptures said He would come back to life again!

From Matthew 28:8; Mark 16:1, 3, 4, 6, 7; Luke 24:1, 3-8, 10; John 20:1-9

86
GREAT DISCOVERY

Mary returned to the tomb and was standing outside crying. As she wept, she stooped and looked in and saw two white-robed angels sitting at the head and foot of the place where the body of Jesus had lain. The angels asked her, "Why are you crying?"

She replied, "Because they have taken away my Lord, and I don't know where they have put Him." She glanced over her shoulder and saw someone standing behind her. It was Jesus, but she didn't recognize Him!

"Why are you crying?" He asked her. "For whom are you looking?"

She thought He was the gardener. "Sir," she said, "if you have taken Him away, tell me where you have put Him, and I will go and get Him."

"Mary!" Jesus said. She turned toward Him.

"Master!" she exclaimed.

"Don't touch Me," He cautioned, "for I haven't yet ascended to the Father. But go find My brothers and tell them that I ascend to My Father and your Father, My God and your God."

It was still early on Sunday morning when Mary Magdalene returned to find the disciples mourning and weeping. She told them that she had seen Jesus, and He was alive! But they didn't believe her!

From Mark 16:9-11; John 20:11-17

87
PLANS FOR A REUNION

As the other women were running from the tomb, suddenly Jesus was there in front of them! "Hello there!" He said. And they fell to the ground before Him, holding His feet, and worshiping Him. Then Jesus said to them, "Don't be frightened! Go tell My brothers to leave at once for Galilee, to meet Me there."

The women returned to Jerusalem and told His eleven disciples—and everyone else—what had happened. But the story sounded like a fairy tale to the men. They didn't believe it.

While the women were on the way into the city, some of the Temple police who were guarding the tomb went and told the chief priests what had happened. A meeting was called with the other Jewish leaders and it was decided to bribe the police to say that Jesus' disciples came during the night while they were asleep and stole His body!

"If the governor hears about it," the council promised, "we'll persuade him to let you alone." So the police accepted the bribe and said what they were told to. Their story spread widely among the Jews, and is still believed by them to this day.

From Matthew 28:9-15; Luke 24:9, 11

88
UNFORGETTABLE JOURNEY

That same day (Sunday) two of Jesus' followers were walking to the village of Emmaus, seven miles out of Jerusalem. As they walked along they were talking of Jesus' death, when suddenly Jesus Himself came along and joined them and began walking beside them! But they didn't recognize Him, for God kept them from doing so.

"You seem to be in a deep discussion about something," He said. "What are you concerned about?"

They stopped short, sadness written across their faces. And one of them, Cleopas, replied, "You must be the only person in all Jerusalem who hasn't heard about the terrible things that happened there last week."

"What things?" Jesus asked.

"The things that happened to Jesus, the Man from Nazareth," they said. "He was a Prophet who did incredible miracles and was a mighty Teacher, highly regarded by both God and man. But the chief priests and

our religious leaders arrested Him and handed Him over to the Roman government to be condemned to death, and they crucified Him.

"But we had thought He was the glorious Messiah and that He had come to rescue Israel. And now—besides all this, which happened three days ago—some women from our group of His followers were at His tomb early this morning and came back with an amazing report that His body was missing and that they had seen some angels there who had told them Jesus is alive! Some of our men ran out to see, and sure enough, Jesus' body was gone, just as the women had said."

Then Jesus said to them, "You are such foolish, foolish people! You find it so hard to believe all that the prophets wrote in the Scriptures! Wasn't it clearly predicted by the prophets that the Messiah would have to suffer these things before entering His time of glory?"

Then Jesus quoted them passage after passage from the writings of the prophets, beginning with the book of Genesis and going right on through the Old Testament, explaining what the passages meant and what they said about Himself.

By this time they were nearing Emmaus and the end of their journey. Jesus would have gone farther, but they begged Him to stay the night with them, as it was getting late. So He went home with them. When they sat down to eat, He asked God's blessing on the food and then took a small loaf of bread and broke it and was passing it over to them, when suddenly—it was as though their eyes were opened—they recognized Him! And at that moment He disappeared!

They began telling each other how their hearts had felt strangely warm as He talked with them, explaining the Scriptures during the walk down the road. Within the hour they were on their way back to Jerusalem.

From Luke 24:13-33

The eleven disciples and the other followers of Jesus greeted the two from Emmaus with these words, "The Lord has really risen! He appeared to Peter!" Then the two told their story of how Jesus had appeared to them as they were walking along and how they had recognized Him as He was breaking the bread. And just as they were telling about it, Jesus Himself was suddenly standing there among them, and He greeted them! But the whole group was terribly frightened, thinking they were seeing a ghost!

"Why are you frightened?" He asked. "Why do you doubt that it is really I? Look at My hands! Look at My feet! You can see that it is I, Myself! Touch Me and make sure that I am not a ghost! For ghosts don't have bodies, as you see that I do!"

As He spoke, He held out His hands for them to see the marks of the nails, and showed them the wounds in His feet. Still they stood there undecided, filled with joy and doubt. Then He asked them, "Do you have anything here to eat?" They gave Him a piece of broiled fish, and He ate it as they watched!

One of the disciples, Thomas (the twin), was not there at the time with the others. So they kept telling him, "We have seen the Lord!"

89
WITHOUT A DOUBT
Sunday evening, April 9, A.D. 30

Sunday, April 16, A.D. 30

But he replied, "I won't believe it unless I see the nail wounds in His hands—and put my fingers into them—and place my hand into His side!"

Eight days later the disciples were together again, and this time Thomas was with them. The doors were locked; but suddenly, as before, Jesus was standing among them and greeting them! Then He said to Thomas, "Put your finger into My hands! Put your hand into My side! Don't be faithless any longer! Believe!"

"My Lord and my God!" Thomas said.

Then Jesus told him, "You believe because you have seen Me. But blessed are those who haven't seen Me and believe anyway."

From Luke 24:34-43; John 20:24-29

90
BREAKFAST ON THE BEACH
April, May, A.D. 30

Later Jesus appeared again to the disciples beside the Lake of Galilee. This is how it happened: A group of them were there—Simon Peter, Thomas (the twin), Nathanael (from Cana, in Galilee), James and John and two other disciples.

Simon Peter said, "I'm going fishing."

"We'll come too," they all said. They went, but caught nothing all night. At dawn they saw a man standing on the beach but couldn't see who it was. He called, "Any fish, boys?"

"No," they replied.

Then He said, "Throw out your net on the right-hand side of the boat, and you'll get plenty of them!" So they did, and couldn't draw in the net because of the weight of the fish, there were so many!

Then John said to Peter, "It is the Lord!" At that, Simon Peter put on his tunic (for he was stripped to the waist) and jumped into the water and swam ashore. The others stayed in the boat and dragged the loaded net to shore, about 300 feet away. When they got there, they saw that a fire was kindled and fish were frying over it, and there was bread.

"Bring some of the fish you've just caught," Jesus said. So Simon Peter went out and pulled the net ashore. He counted 153 large fish; and yet the net hadn't torn!

"Now come and have some breakfast!" Jesus said; and none of them dared ask Him if He really was the Lord for they were quite sure of it. Then Jesus went around serving the bread and fish.

This was the third time Jesus had appeared to them since His return from the dead.

From John 21:1-14

91

PLANS REVEALED

May 19, A.D. 30

Then the eleven disciples went to the mountain where Jesus had told them to meet Him. There they met Him and worshiped Him—but some of them weren't sure it really was Jesus!

Jesus told the disciples, "All authority in heaven and earth has been given to Me. Therefore go and make disciples in all the nations, baptizing them into the name of the Father and of the Son and of the Holy Spirit, and teaching them to obey all the commands I have given you. Be sure of this—that I am with you always, even to the end of the world."

Then He also said, "When I was with you before, do you not remember My telling you that everything writ-

ten about Me by Moses and the prophets and in the Psalms must all come true?"

At last, He opened their minds to understand these many Scriptures! As Jesus continued to speak He said, "Yes, it was written long ago that the Messiah must suffer and die and rise again from the dead on the third day; and that this message of salvation should be taken to all nations, starting from Jerusalem: (There is forgiveness of sins for all who turn to Me.) You have seen these prophecies come true, and now I will send the Holy Spirit upon you, just as My Father promised. Don't begin telling others yet. Stay here in the city until He comes and fills you with power from heaven."

Then Jesus led them out along the road to Bethany, and lifting His hands to heaven, He blessed them. It was not long afterwards that He rose into the sky and disappeared into a cloud, leaving them staring after Him. And they worshiped Him.

As they were straining their eyes for another glimpse, suddenly two white-robed men were standing there among them, and they said, "Men of Galilee, why are you standing here staring at the sky? Jesus has gone away to heaven, and some day, just as He went, He will return!"

They were at the Mount of Olives at the time, so now they walked the half mile back to Jerusalem filled with mighty joy, and held a prayer meeting in an upstairs room of the house where they were staying.

After May 29, A.D. 30 The disciples went everywhere preaching (after the Holy Spirit came to them—as Jesus had promised). The Lord was with them and confirmed what they said by the miracles that followed their messages.

From Matthew 28:16-20; Mark 16:20; Luke 24:44-50, 52; Acts 1:9-14

92
THE REASON WHY

Jesus' disciples saw Him do many other miracles besides the ones told about in this book, but these are recorded so that you will believe that He is the Messiah, the Son of God, and that believing in Him you will have Life.

And I suppose that if all the other events in Jesus' life were written, the whole world could hardly contain the books!

From John 20:30, 31; 21:25